THE VOCATION OF MAN

The Library of Liberal Arts
OSKAR PIEST, FOUNDER

THE VOCATION
OF MAN

JOHANN GOTTLIEB FICHTE

Edited, with an introduction, by
RODERICK M. CHISHOLM

The Library of Liberal Arts
published by
Bobbs-Merrill Educational Publishing
Indianapolis

Johann Gottlieb Fichte: 1762-1814

THE VOCATION OF MAN was originally published in 1800

· · · · · · · · · · · · · · · · · · ·

Copyright © 1956 by The Bobbs-Merrill Company, Inc.

Printed in the United States of America

The Bobbs-Merrill Company, Inc.
4300 West 62nd Street
Indianapolis, Indiana 46268

Eighth Printing—1981
Library of Congress Catalog Card Number: 56-44104

ISBN 0-672-60220-2

CONTENTS

· · · · · · · · · · · · · · · · ·

THE VOCATION OF MAN

INTRODUCTION

In *The Vocation of Man*, Johann Gottlieb Fichte attempts to lead us "from the world of sense into a region beyond it." His book is written for people unfamiliar with the more technical discussions of philosophers; as a result it is one of the clearest introductions to the "idealistic" philosophy of nineteenth-century Germany.

The argument of *The Vocation of Man* is essentially this: If we were to consider only what seems to be the position of man in nature, we would be led to a false conception of man. We would be led to suppose that he is a product of natural forces, both physiologically and psychologically, and that all of his actions, like other physical events, are the inevitable results of the conditions under which they happen to occur. But if we consider the way in which we come to *know* the physical world, we will find that this world is a product of our own mental activity. And if we take seriously the demands of our moral consciousness, we will see that in the "true world"—a world which transcends nature—"human existence is one with the Divine."

In studying nature, we assume that, for every event, there is some set of causal conditions which are antecedent to it and which determine it completely. We assume, in other words, that every natural event takes place under conditions such that, *without* those conditions, the event would not occur and, *with* those conditions, it would not fail to occur. And we assume that the conditions are themselves events or states of affairs which, in turn, are completely determined by still other events or states of affairs. In Book I of *The Vocation of Man*, Fichte raises doubts about the existence of *moral* responsibility in a system of things which thus conforms to the principle of causality. If our

vii

assumptions, expressing this principle, are true and if man is a "link in this chain of the rigid necessity of Nature," then it can be said of all of his actions that they, too, are completely determined by the conditions under which they occur. If a man steals, for example, then he must have been so conditioned physiologically and psychologically that, when the moment came, he stole necessarily and there was nothing else he could have done instead. From this, according to Fichte, it would follow that the source of our actions is the whole system of nature and that we ourselves are not responsible for what we do. And this conclusion, Fichte believes, is intolerable. Our moral consciousness tells us that our actions proceed, not from causal antecedents which are independent of us, but from ourselves alone.

In order to see the true relation between our actions and the system of nature, according to Fichte, we must first consider that which we take to be our *knowledge* of nature.

We believe that, by means of sight, touch, hearing, and the other senses, we can perceive things which are external to us. Fichte tries to show in Book II that this belief is mistaken. He points out, first, that what we take to be our perception of external things is something dependent on our knowledge of ourselves. If a man claims to see a tower in the center of the market place, this claim is based on his immediate apprehension of what he sees—or, better, of what he *thinks* he sees—when he believes himself to be near the market place and looking into its center. In knowing what it is that he thinks he sees, the man knows something about *himself;* hence, according to Fichte's reasoning, we can say that "in all perception you perceive in the first place only yourself and your own condition."

What is the nature of that private condition upon which external perception thus depends? Whenever you think you perceive something, according to Fichte, you apprehend certain sensible qualities—colors, sounds, feelings of touch, and the like—which you *attribute* to the external object you think you perceive. Fichte also expresses this conclusion by saying that, when you think you perceive an external object, you are in fact aware only of certain sensible qualities which you take to *signify* that object. He had said, above, that "in all perception you perceive *in the first place* only yourself and your own condition." But he now says, even more paradoxically, "in all perception you perceive *only* your own condition."

The validity of this reasoning had been challenged, in the previous century, by Thomas Reid, who attributed it to Bishop Berkeley; Reid's attack has been revived in the twentieth century. But the argument seemed obviously cogent to Fichte, as it did to subsequent idealists. In the first book of *The World as Will and Idea*, Schopenhauer reasons similarly in defense of the doctrine that "the World is my idea."

Given his paradoxical conclusion—that in all perception we perceive only our own condition—Fichte goes on to ask: What justification do we have for supposing that the sensible qualities, which are the only objects of our immediate knowledge, are in fact *reliable* signs of external objects? Or, more briefly, what justification do we have for supposing that there is a world of nature at all?

One possible answer is that, in taking sensible qualities to be signs of external objects, we are reasoning from effect to cause: we assume that our sensations must have some cause and we then infer, in particular cases, that the cause is this or that external object. The assumption that our sensations must have some cause depends upon the more general principle, mentioned above, that every event must have some cause. But, Fichte now asks, what is the justification for this more general principle? What reason can be given for supposing that every event has a cause? This question leads to another of Fichte's characteristic doctrines.

We have no *immediate* apprehension of the truth of this principle, for we have seen (Fichte supposes) that our immediate knowledge does not extend beyond our apprehension of sensible qualities. Is the principle inferred from something else we know? Ordinarily, if a man were called upon to defend his acceptance of the causal principle, he would point out that the objects in nature do in fact conform to this principle. But, in the present context, this defense would be circular. If it is by means of the principle of causality that we arrive at our belief in an external world of nature, then it cannot be by means of our beliefs about external things that we arrive at our belief in the principle of causality. "Shall the earth rest on the great elephant and the great elephant again rest upon the earth?"

If the principle of causality is not known immediately and if we cannot justify our acceptance of it by reference to beliefs about external things, we must conclude, according to Fichte, that the principle is an "inward law of thought." Although we say it is impossible for there to be an event which has no cause, this impossibility, Fichte proposes, concerns not external objects or our sensations, but the way in which we think. Instead of saying that it is impossible for there to be an event which has no cause, we could say, more accurately, that it is impossible for us to *suppose* that any event occurs without supposing also that the event has a cause. Fichte is here applying one of the principles of Kant's "Copernican revolution" in philosophy. Copernicus had attributed the ostensible turning of the firmament to the actual turning of the observer. Kant—and Fichte—attribute the ostensible causal order of the world to the way in which the subject must *think* the world.

We can now say, according to Fichte, that what we take to be our knowledge of external things is in fact only a knowledge of our own mental activity. "What you assume to be a consciousness of an object is nothing but a consciousness of the fact that you have *posited* the object—posited it necessarily, in accordance with an inward law of your thought, at the same time as the sensation." The object which you thus suppose to exist is "a product of your own thought only." In Fichte's most important work, the *Grundlage der gesamten Wissenschaftslehre,* he describes this mental activity by saying that, in having a sensation, the subject, or Ego, necessarily posits the existence of a non-Ego, something other than itself *("Das Ich setzt das Nicht-Ich").*

We cannot experience our own selves any more directly than we can experience external objects, for the only objects of immediate experience, according to Fichte's reasoning, are sensible qualities. "Strictly speaking, I ought to say 'The thought appears *(es erscheint der Gedanke)* that I feel, perceive, think,' and not 'I feel, perceive, think.'" But Fichte argues, as Kant had done in the *Critique of Pure Reason,* that it is impossible for there to be an experience unless it is accompanied by the thought of a subject which is *having* that experience. Sensations are thus accompanied both with the thought of an object and with the thought of a subject. Hence the Ego not only posits the non-Ego—it posits itself as well. *("Das Ich setzt sich selbst.")* [1]

Fichte now returns to his original problem concerning the status of moral responsibility. His problem, it will be recalled, was that of reconciling what we seem to know about the causal order of nature with what we seem to learn from our moral consciousness. Our moral consciousness tells us that we alone are responsible for our acts; the study of nature tells us that every event is the inevitable

---

[1] "Positing," according to Fichte, is a type of mental activity which is not conscious but which takes place according to *dialectical* principles. In the *Wissenschaftslehre,* he describes the dialectic of thought in detail, making use of the terms "thesis," "antithesis," and "synthesis." These concepts, but not the terms themselves, were later to figure prominently in Hegel's philosophy. Hegel shared Fichte's belief that, in order to understand the world, it is essential to "think dialectically."

and necessary consequence of its causal antecedents and hence that every man's behavior, if it takes place within nature, is determined by the conditions under which he happens to find himself. But we now see, Fichte believes, that nature itself is our own creation—and this insight suggests a solution to our problem. Once you are made aware of the true status of nature, "you will no longer tremble at a necessity which exists only in your own thought; no longer fear to be crushed by things which are the product of your own mind; no longer place yourself, the thinking being, in the same class with the thoughts which proceed from you."

But we are now left with a very different problem. By studying the nature of knowledge, we have been led to the conviction that we can know nothing but our own mental states. Hence we have yet to attain a reality which "lies beyond mere appearance." In Book III, Fichte tells how reality is to be apprehended.

Fichte felt that, in discussing the nature of knowledge in Book II, he had carried the principles of Kant's *Critique of Pure Reason* to their proper conclusion. In Book III, he appeals to the insight of Kant's *Critique of Practical Reason:* the solution to our philosophical problem is to be found, not by further consideration of nature or of our ostensible knowledge of nature, but by accepting the deliverance of our *moral* consciousness.

The moral consciousness reveals to each of us that we have duties to *act* in certain ways toward ourselves and toward others. If we are to take these revelations seriously —and the man who is truly moral, according to Fichte, cannot do otherwise—we will believe that they pertain to a "real world"; we will have *faith* that there is a world in which our duties can be performed and our obligations fulfilled. But we have seen that the world of sense is no more than a "system of pictures." Therefore—since our moral activity cannot exist merely to serve the purposes of the world of pictures—there is "a supersensual world whose purposes it does promote." This insight into two orders—"the one purely spiritual, in which I rule by my will alone; the other sensuous, in which I operate by my deed"—comes to us only by means of our moral consciousness. Fichte elsewhere speaks of the sensible world as a world of obstacles which the subject has put in its own way in order that it may practice virtue; our world is the material for our duty made manifest to the senses *(unsere Welt is das versinnlichte Material unserer Pflicht).*

The latter half of Book III is a sermon, some of it obscure, on the vocation of man. A more prosaic statement of the same subject is to be found in Fichte's *Addresses to the German Nation.* These addresses, delivered in Berlin during the winter of 1807 and 1808, were intended to reawaken the spirit of the German people after the defeat of Prussia by Napoleon in 1806 and 1807. In the third address, Fichte summarizes his conception of what should be taught in an adequate system of national education:

> The pupil of this education is not merely a member of human society here on this earth and for the short span of life which is permitted him on it. He is also, and is undoubtedly acknowledged by education to be, a link in the eternal chain of spiritual life in a higher social order. A training which has undertaken to include the whole of his being should undoubtedly lead him to a knowledge of this higher order also. Just as it led him to sketch out for himself, by his own activity, an image of that moral world order which never is, but always is to be, so must it lead him to create in thought by the same self-activity an image of that supersensuous world order in which nothing becomes, and which never has become, but which simply is forever; all this in such a way that he intimately understands and perceives that it could not be otherwise. Under proper guidance he will complete his attempts at such an image, and find at the end that nothing really exists but life, the spiritual life which lives in thought, and that other things do not really exist, but only appear to exist. The reason for this appearance, a

reason that results from thought, he will likewise grasp, even if only in general. Further, he will perceive that, amid the various forms which it received, not by chance, but according to a law founded in God Himself, the spiritual life which alone really exists is one, the divine life itself, which exists and manifests itself only in living thought. He will thus learn to know and keep holy his own and every other spiritual life as an eternal link in the chain of the manifestation of the divine life. Only in immediate contact with God and in the direct emanation of his life from Him will he find life, light, and happiness, but in any separation from that immediate contact, death, darkness, and misery.

In considering the knowledge of nature, Fichte was led to the conclusion that the physical things we think we perceive are a product of our own mental activity. By similar reasoning we might conclude that other people, other "rational beings," are also a product of this activity—a part of what it posited by the subject or Ego. But, Fichte states, we must appeal once again to the moral consciousness. And the moral consciousness tells us that we must treat other people, not as mere pictures resulting from our own thought, but as free and independent beings like ourselves. Moreover, if we are truly moral, we will restrict our own freedom for the sake of the freedom and the moral activity of others. "It is the vocation of our species to unite itself into one single body, all the parts of which shall be thoroughly known to each other, and all possessed of similar culture." [2]

[2] In the *Science of Rights*, Fichte applies his ethical principles in detail to law, the family, the rights of individuals within the state, and the relations between states. "The state in itself," he there says, "is nothing but an abstract conception; only the citizens, as such, are actual persons." The state exists primarily to preserve the rights of its citizens; but eventually, Fichte argues, states must confederate themselves in order to secure the freedom of all men. The members of this confederation will agree to the following compact: "We promise to exterminate with united force any state, whether it belong to this confederation or not, which shall refuse to recognize the independence

Fichte's final conclusion, in *The Vocation of Man*, is that God is the foundation for the moral order of the world and that each of us exists "only in God and through God." He concedes that this conclusion is difficult to grasp intellectually; it concerns a subject matter proper to the moral consciousness rather than to the understanding.

In *The Way Toward the Blessed Life*, Fichte argues that, if we consider the nature of being *(Sein)* as such, we see that it cannot change, that it cannot come into being or pass away, and that it must be *one*. All things are contained in the one true Being, which Fichte calls God, the Word, or the Absolute. Since the Divine Existence is infinite, it cannot be conceived anthropomorphically; we cannot attribute intelligence or personality to it, nor can we even conceive of it as a particular substance. Like Kant, Fichte rejects the usual arguments purporting to demonstrate God's existence. We cannot appeal to the principle of causality, for example, because this principle, as we have seen, is merely "an inward law of thought." Design, similarly, is a subjective concept which cannot be extended beyond the world of appearance. And we cannot say that God *created* the world. The notion of a creation *ex nihilo* is the "fundamental error of Judaism as well as of Heathenism"; creation is incompatible with the Divine Nature (for the Being of God includes everything that there is) and is, in the strictest sense, absurd. The true Christian God, according to Fichte, is not the creator described in Genesis, but the Word—or *Logos*—described in the Gospel according to St. John.

Fichte's critics accused him of atheism. His reply was that the God he describes may be identified with the moral order *(moralische Ordnung)* of the world. He admitted that this is a conception of God which "must be believed in, not inferred." It is a conception which is beyond the reach of

of any one of us, or which shall violate a treaty concluded between it and one of us." Ultimately, according to Fichte, all men should be united in a single commonwealth.

our science; but science itself, in assuming the existence of a world of things, rests upon *faith*. "Faith is the ground of all conviction, scientific or moral." The following passage appears in his paper entitled, "On the Definition of the Idea of Religion," written in 1798:

> It is an error to say that it is doubtful whether or not there is a God. It is not doubtful, but the most certain of all certainties—nay, the foundation of all other certainties—the one absolutely valid objective truth—that there is a moral order in the world; that to every rational being is assigned his particular place in that order, and the work which he has to do; that his destiny, in so far as it is not occasioned by his own conduct, is the result of this plan; that in no other way can even a hair fall from his head, nor a sparrow fall to the ground around him; that every true and good action prospers, and every bad action fails; and that all things must work together for good to those who truly love goodness. On the other hand, no one who reflects a moment, and honestly avows the result of his reflection, can remain in doubt that the conception of God as a *particular substance* is impossible and contradictory: and it is right candidly to say this, and to silence the babbling of the schools, in order that the true religion of cheerful virtue may be established in its place.

If Being is one, unchanging and self-sufficient, why is it that there *seems* to be a world in which there are many things and persons, all of them independent and subject to change? In the *Wissenschaftslehre*, Fichte attempts to answer this question by considering the essential nature of Being, or God, and deducing its properties. There he tells us why it is essential to Being that it have a manifestation *(Äusserung)* in which it recognizes itself as a power under an obligation to realize itself, why in this manifestation there seem to be a multiplicity of individual subjects, or selves, each of whom posits the same world of material things in space and time, and why the true vocation of each of these individuals is to lead a moral life in which the Divine

Existence "becomes visible to itself." But unless the reader can grasp the concept of the *manifestation* of Being, Fichte's deductions are almost impossible to follow.

The most difficult concept in Fichte's philosophy is that of "the absolute unity of Human Existence with the Divine." In God's manifestation, we are distinct from each other and from God; but in the "true world" we are one with God and hence also with each other. In attempting to explicate his doctrine, Fichte inevitably falls back upon metaphors. He sometimes suggests that particular things are related to the one, true Being as links are related to a chain or notes to a melody. Sometimes he compares manifestation with the action of a prism whereby pure and colorless light is broken up into many separate hues. But these metaphors must not mislead us into thinking that the manifestation of Being involves the relation of whole to part or that of causal interaction. For, according to Fichte's doctrine, true Being is one and therefore has no parts, and causation applies, not to reality, but to the way in which we think. In the end, Fichte concedes that the relation whereby particular selves become one with the Absolute is "the one great mystery of the invisible world."

RODERICK M. CHISHOLM

SELECTED BIBLIOGRAPHY

Fichte's Principal Works

Versuch einer Kritik aller Offenbarung (1792)
Grundlage der gesamten Wissenschaftslehre (1794)
Grundlagen des Naturrechtes nach den Prinzipien der Wissenschaftslehre (1796)
System der Sittenlehre nach den Prinzipien der Wissenschaftslehre (1798)
Die Bestimmung des Menschen (1800)
Der geschlossene Handelsstaat (1800)
Die Anweisung zum seligen Leben (1806)
Reden an die deutsche Nation (1808)

English Translations of Fichte's Works

The Science of Knowledge. Translated by A. E. Kroeger, Philadelphia, 1868
The Science of Rights. Translated by A. E. Kroeger, Philadelphia, 1869
Addresses to the German Nation. Translated by R. F. Jones and G. H. Turnbull, Chicago, 1922
The Popular Works of Johann Gottlieb Fichte. 2 vols. Translated by William Smith, London, 1889. These volumes include *The Vocation of Man*

Collateral Reading

Royce, Josiah, *The Spirit of Modern Philosophy*, Cambridge, Mass., 1931
Royce, Josiah, *Lectures on Modern Idealism*, New Haven, 1934
Fischer, Kuno, *Geschichte der Neueren Philosophie*, Vol. VI, Heidelberg, 1923

NOTE ON THE TEXT

Die Bestimmung des Menschen was first published in Berlin in 1800. It appears in Volume II of Fichte's *Sämtliche Werke* (Berlin, 1845-46), edited by Immanuel Hermann Fichte, and in Volume III of Fichte's *Werke* (Leipzig, 1908-12), edited by Fritz Medicus. William Smith's translation was first published in London in 1848; it appeared in revised form in 1889, in Volume I of the fourth edition of the *Popular Works of Johann Gottlieb Fichte,* edited and translated by Smith.

In the present edition, Smith's translation has been thoroughly revised and spelling, capitalization, and punctuation have been modernized in accordance with present-day American usage. Revisions were made with reference to the Medicus edition of Fichte. The expression *"ausser mir"* has been translated throughout as "external to me." The Editor's footnotes have been bracketed.

R. M. C.

THE VOCATION OF MAN

FOREWORD

This work has for its subject matter that part of the new philosophy which is of use outside the schools, set forth in that order in which it would naturally present itself to unsophisticated thought. The more profound arguments by which subtle objections and extravagances of overrefined minds are to be met fall beyond the limits of our task; so, too, whatever is but the foundation of some other positive science, and whatever belongs to pedagogy in its widest sense, that is, to the deliberate and arbitrary education of the human race. The objections are not made by the natural understanding; positive science we leave to professional scholars; and the education of the human race, in so far as that depends upon human effort, we leave to its appointed teachers and statesmen.

This book, therefore, is not intended for professional philosophers, for they will find nothing in it that has not been already set forth in other writings of the same author. It ought to be intelligible to all readers who are able to understand a book at all. To those who wish only to repeat, in somewhat varied order, certain phrases which they have already learned by rote, and who mistake this business of the memory for understanding, it will doubtless be found unintelligible.

This book is intended to attract and animate the reader, and to elevate him from the world of sense into a region beyond it; at least the author is conscious that he has not entered upon his task without such inspiration. Often, indeed, the fire with which we commence an undertaking disappears during the toil of execution; and thus, at the conclusion of a work, we are in danger of doing ourselves injustice upon this point. In short, whether the author has

3

succeeded in attaining his object or not can be determined only by the effect which the work shall produce on the readers to whom it is addressed, and in this the author has no voice.

I must, however, remind my reader that the "I" who speaks in this book is not the author himself; it is the author's wish that the reader will himself assume this character. And it is to be hoped that the reader—instead of resting content merely with an historical apprehension of what is here said—will actually hold converse with himself during the reading, will deliberate, draw conclusions and form resolutions, like his imaginary representative, and thus, by his own labor and reflection, develop and build up within himself that mode of thought the mere picture of which is presented to him in the book.

BOOK ONE

DOUBT

I believe that I am now acquainted with no inconsiderable part of the world that surrounds me, and I have certainly employed sufficient labor and care in the acquisition of this knowledge. I have put faith only in the concurrent testimony of my senses, only in repeated and unvarying experience; what I have seen, I have touched, and what I have touched, I have analyzed. I have repeated my observations again and again. I have compared the various phenomena with each other and I have been satisfied only when I could understand their mutual connection, when I could explain and deduce the one from the other, when I could calculate the result beforehand, and the observation of the result had proved the accuracy of my calculations. Therefore, I am now as well assured of the accuracy of this part of my knowledge as of my own existence; I walk with a firm step in these understood spheres of my world, and do actually every moment venture welfare and life itself on the certainty of my convictions.

But—what am I myself, and what is my vocation?

Superfluous question! It is long since I have been completely instructed upon these points, and it would take much time to repeat all the details I have heard, learned, and believed concerning them.

And in what way then have I attained this knowledge, which I have this dim remembrance of acquiring? Have I, impelled by a burning desire of knowledge, toiled on through uncertainty, doubt, and contradiction? Have I, when any belief was presented to me, withheld my assent until I had examined and re-examined, sifted and com-

pared it—until an inward voice proclaimed to me, irresistibly and without the possibility of doubt, "Thus it is—thus
only—as surely as you live and breathe." No! I remember no
such state of mind. Those instructions were put to me
before I sought them, the answers were given before I had
put the questions. I heard, for I could not avoid doing so,
and what was taught me remained in my memory just as
chance had disposed it; without examination and without
interest I allowed everything to take its place in my mind.

How then could I persuade myself that I possessed any
real knowledge upon these matters? If I know that only of
which I am convinced, which I have myself discovered, myself experienced, then I cannot truly say that I possess
even the slightest knowledge of my vocation. I know only
what others assert they know about it, and all that I am
really sure of is that I have heard this or that said upon
the subject.

Thus, although I have myself inquired into trivial matters with care and attention, I have relied wholly upon
the word of others in matters of importance. I have supposed that others have had, for the highest affairs of humanity, an earnest and exact concern which I have by no means
discovered in myself. I have esteemed them indescribably
higher than myself.

Whatever truth they really possess, where can they have
learned it other than through their own reflection? And
why may not I, by means of the same reflection, discover
the like truth for myself, since I too have a being as well
as they? How much have I hitherto undervalued and
slighted myself!

It shall be no longer so. From this moment I will enter
on my rights and assume the dignity that belongs to me.
External aids will be cast aside. I will examine for myself.
If any secret wishes concerning the result of my inquiries,
any partial leaning toward certain conclusions stir within
me, I will forget and renounce them; and I will not let

them influence the direction of my thoughts. I will perform my task with firmness and integrity; I will honestly accept the result whatever it may be. What I find to be truth, let it sound as it may, shall be welcome to me. I will *know*. With the same certainty with which I am assured that this ground will support me when I tread on it, that this fire will burn me if I approach too near to it, will I know what I am and what I shall be. And should it prove impossible for me to know this, then I will know at least that I cannot know it. Even to this conclusion of my inquiry will I submit, should it approve itself to me as the truth. I hasten to the completion of my task.

I seize on Nature in its rapid flight, detain it for an instant and hold the present moment steadily in view; I reflect upon this Nature within which my thinking powers have hitherto been developed and trained to those researches that belong to her domain.

I am surrounded by objects which I am compelled to regard as separate, independent, self-subsisting wholes. I behold plants, trees, animals. To each individual I ascribe certain properties and attributes by which I distinguish it from others; to this plant, such a form; to that plant, another; to this tree, leaves of one shape; to that tree, leaves of another.

Every object has its appointed number of attributes, neither more nor less. To every question, whether it is this or that, there is, for anyone who is thoroughly acquainted with it, a decisive Yes possible, or a decisive No—so that there is an end of all doubt or hesitation on the subject. Everything that exists *is* something, or it *is not* this something; is colored, or is not colored; has a certain color, or has it not, may be tasted, or may not; is tangible, or is not; and so on, *ad infinitum*.

Every object possesses each of these attributes in a definite degree. Let a measure be given for any of its attributes;

then we may discover the exact extent of that attribute, which it neither exceeds nor falls short of. I measure the height of this tree; it is defined, and it is not a single line higher or lower than it is. I consider the green of its leaves; it is a definite green, not the smallest shade darker or lighter, fresher or more faded than it is; although I may have neither measure nor expression for these qualities. I turn my eye to this plant; it is at a definite stage of growth between its budding and its maturity, not in the smallest degree nearer or more remote from either than it is. *Everything that exists is determined throughout; it is what it is, and nothing else.*

Not that I am unable to conceive of an object as floating unattached between opposite determinations. I do certainly conceive of indefinite objects; for more than half of my thoughts consist of such conceptions. I think of a tree *in general.* Has this tree fruit or not, leaves or not; if it has, what is their number? What kind of a tree is it? How large is it? And so on. All these questions remain unanswered, and my thought is undetermined in these respects; for I did not propose to myself the thought of any particular tree, but of a tree generally. But in leaving the tree thus undetermined, I deprive it of any possibility of existing. Everything that actually exists has its determinate number of all the possible attributes of actual existence, and each of these in a determinate measure, as surely as it actually exists, even though I may not be able to exhaust the properties of any one object, or to apply to them any standard of measurement.

But Nature pursues its course of ceaseless change, and, while I speak, the moment I sought to hold before me is gone, and all is changed; before I could lay hold of it, everything was different. It had not always been as it was when I observed it; it had *become* so.

Why then, and from what cause, had it become so? Why had Nature, amid the infinite variety of possible forms, assumed in this moment precisely these and no others?

For this reason: that they were preceded precisely by those conditions which did precede them, and by no others; and because the present could arise out of those and out of no other possible conditions. Had anything in the preceding moment been in the smallest degree different from what it was, then in the present moment something would have been different from what it is. And from what cause were all things in that preceding moment precisely such as they were? For this reason: that in the moment preceding that, they were such as they were then. And this moment again was dependent on its predecessor, and that on another, and so on into the past without limit. In like manner will Nature, in the next moment, be necessarily determined to the particular forms which it will then assume—for this reason, that in the present moment it is determined exactly as it is; and were anything in the present moment in the smallest degree different from what it is, then in the succeeding moment something would necessarily be different from what it will be. And in the moment following that, all things will be precisely as they will be, because in the immediately previous moment they will be as they will be; and so will *its* successor proceed forth from it, and another from that, and so on into the future without limit.

Nature proceeds throughout the whole infinite series of her possible determinations without pause; and the succession of these changes is not arbitrary, but follows strict and unalterable laws. Whatever exists in Nature, necessarily exists as it does exist, and it is absolutely impossible that it should be otherwise. I enter within an unbroken chain of phenomena in which every link is determined by that which has preceded it, and in its turn determines the next; so that, were I able to trace into the past the causes through which alone any given moment could have come into actual existence, and to follow out in the future the consequences which must necessarily flow from it, then, at that moment, and by means of thought alone, I could discover all possible conditions of the universe, both past and future—past, by explaining the given moment; future, by predicting its consequences. In every point I experience the whole, for *only* through the whole is each part what it is; but through this it is *necessarily* what it is.

What is it then that I have found? If I review my assertions as a whole, I find their substance to be this: that in every stage of development an antecedent is necessarily supposed, from which and through which alone that stage has arisen; in every condition another condition is supposed; in every existence, another existence; and that from nothing, nothing whatever can proceed.

Let me pause here a little, and develop whatever is contained in this principle, until it becomes perfectly clear to me! For it may well be that the whole success of my future inquiry depends upon a clear insight into this point.

Why, and from what cause, I had asked, are the determinate forms of objects precisely such as they are at this moment. I assumed without further proof, and without the slightest inquiry, as an absolute, immediate, certain and unalterable truth, that they had a cause—that they had attained existence and reality, not through themselves, but through something which lay beyond them. I found their existence insufficient to account for itself, and I was compelled to assume another existence beyond them, as a necessary condition of theirs. But why did I find the existence of these qualities and determinate forms insufficient for itself? Why did I find it to be an incomplete existence? What was there in it which betrayed to me its insufficiency? Without doubt, it was this: in the first place, these qualities do not exist in and for themselves; they are qualities *of* something else, attributes of a substance, forms of something formed; and the supposition of such a substance, of a something to support these attributes—of a *substratum* for them, to use the phraseology of the Schools—is a necessary condition of conceiving such qualities. Further, in attributing a definite quality to such a *substratum*, I assume the thing to be in a state of rest or repose and not in a state of change or of becoming. Were I to regard it as in a state of transition, then there could be no definite determination, but merely an endless series of changes from one state to another. The state of determination in a thing is thus a state and expression of mere passivity; and a state of mere passivity is in itself an incomplete existence. Such passivity itself demands an activity to which it may be referred, by which it can be explained, and through which it first becomes conceivable—or, as we would ordinarily say, an activity *which contains the ground of this passivity.*

Thus what I found myself compelled to assume was *not* that the various and successive determinations of Nature themselves produce each other; it was not that the present determination annihilates itself, and, in the next moment, when it no longer exists, produces another, which is different from itself, and not contained in it, to fill its place. For this is wholly inconceivable. The mere determination produces neither itself nor anything else.

What I found myself compelled to assume in order to account for the gradual origin and the changes of those determinations, was an *active power,* peculiar to the object, and constituting its essential nature.

And how, then, do I conceive of this power? What is its nature, and the modes of its manifestation? This only: that under these definite conditions it produces, by its own energy and for its own sake, this definite effect and no other, and that it produces this certainly and infallibly.

This principle of activity, of independent and spontaneous development, exists in itself alone, and in nothing beyond itself, as surely as it is power—power which is not compelled or set in motion. The cause of its having developed itself precisely in this manner and no other lies partly in itself—because it is this particular power and no other—and partly in the circumstances under which it develops itself. Both of these—the inward determination of a power by itself, and its outward determination by circumstances—must be united in order to produce a change. The outward circumstances, the passive condition of things, can of itself produce no change, for it has within it the opposite of all change: inert existence. The *power* is wholly determined, for only on this condition is it conceivable; but its determination is completed only through the circumstances under which it is developed. I can conceive of a power—it can have an existence for me—only in so far as I can perceive an effect proceeding from it; an inactive power—which should yet be a *power,* and not an inert *thing*—is wholly inconceivable. Every effect, however, is determined; and, since the effect is but the expression, but another mode of the activity itself, the active power is made determinable in its activity; and the ground of this determination lies partly in itself, for it cannot otherwise be conceived of as a particular and definite power, and partly outside of itself, because its own determination can be conceived only as conditioned by something else.

A flower has sprung out of the earth, and I infer from thence a formative power in Nature. Such a formative power exists for me only so far as this flower and others, plants generally, and animals, exist for me. I can describe this power only through its effects, and it is to me no more than that which brings about such effects—the generative principle of flowers, plants, animals, and organic forms in general. I will go further and maintain that a flower, and this particular flower, could arise in this place only in so far as all other circumstances united to make it possible. The flower is not possible without the union of all these circumstances. But if the flower is actually to exist, some-thing more is needed. I must assume that there is a partic-ular power in Nature—a power which is spontaneous and original and one which is determinate in that it produces a *flower*. Any other power of Nature under the same circum-stances might have produced something entirely different. I have thus reached the following view of the Universe.

When I contemplate all things as one whole, one Nature, there is but one power. When I regard them as separate existences, there are many powers which develop themselves according to their inward laws and pass through all the pos-sible forms of which they are capable; all objects in Nature are but those powers under certain determinate forms. The manifestations of each individual power of Nature become what they are—are determined—partly by the essential character of the power itself, and partly through the mani-festations of all the other powers of Nature with which it is connected; but it is connected with them all, for Nature is one connected whole. The individual powers of Nature, therefore, are unalterably determined; while the essential character of each power remains what it is, and while the power continues to manifest itself under these particular circumstances, its manifestations must necessarily be what they are; it is absolutely impossible that they should be in the smallest degree different from what they are.

In every moment of her duration Nature is one connected whole; in every moment each individual part must be what it is, because all the others are what they are; and you could not remove a single grain of sand from its place with-out thereby (although perhaps imperceptibly to you) chang-ing something throughout all parts of the immeasurable whole. But *every moment of this duration is determined by all past moments, and will determine every future moment;* and you cannot conceive even the position of a grain of sand other than as it is in the *present,* without being compelled to conceive the whole indefinite *past* to have been other than what it has been, and the whole indefinite *future* to be other than what it will be. Make the experiment, for instance, with this grain of sand. Suppose it to lie some few paces further inland than it does—then the stormwind that drove it in from the sea must have been stronger than it actually was; then the preceding state of the weather, by which this wind was occasioned and its degree of strength determined must have been different from what it actually was; and the previous state by which this particular weather was determined, and so on; and thus you have, without stay or limit, a wholly different temperature of the air from that which really existed, and a different constitution of the bodies which possess an influence over this temperature, and over which, on the other hand, it exercises such an influence. On the fruitfulness or unfruitfulness of countries, and through that, or even directly, on the duration of human life, this temperature exercises a most decided influence. How can you know—since it is not permitted us to penetrate the arcana of Nature, and it is therefore allowable to speak of possibilities—how can you know that in such a state of weather as may have been necessary to carry this grain of sand a few paces further inland, some one of your forefathers might not have perished from hunger, or cold, or heat, before begetting that son from whom you are descended; and that thus you might never have been at all, and all that you have ever done, and all that you ever hope to do in this world, must have been obstructed in order that a grain of sand might lie in a different place?

I myself, with all that I call mine, am a link in this chain of the rigid necessity of Nature. There was a time—so others tell me who were then alive, and I am compelled by reasoning to admit such a time of which I am not immediately conscious—there was a time in which I was not, and a moment in which I began to be. I then existed only for others, and not yet for myself. Since then, my self, my self-consciousness, has gradually unfolded itself, and I have discovered in myself certain capacities and faculties, wants, and natural desires. I am a definite creature, which came into being at a certain time.

I have not come into being by my own power. It would be the highest absurdity to suppose that I existed before I came into existence, in order to bring myself into existence. I have, then, been called into being by another power beyond myself. And by what power but the universal power of Nature, since I too am a part of Nature? The time at which my existence began, and the attributes with which I came into being, were determined by this universal power of Nature; and all the forms under which these inborn attributes have since manifested themselves, and will manifest themselves as long as I have a being, are determined by the same power. It was impossible that, instead of me, another should have come into existence; it is impossible that this being, once here, should at any moment of its existence be other than what it is and will be.

That my successive states of being have been accompanied by consciousness, and that some of them, such as thoughts, resolutions, and the like, appear to be nothing but varied modes of consciousness, need not perplex my reasonings. It is the natural constitution of the plant to develop itself, of the animal to move, and of man to think. Why should I hesitate to acknowledge the last as the manifestation of an original power of Nature, as well as the first and second? Nothing could hinder me from doing so but mere wonder, thought being assuredly a far higher and more subtle operation of Nature than the formation of a plant or the proper motion of an animal. But how can I accord to such a feeling any influence whatever upon the calm conclusions of reason? I cannot indeed explain how the power of Nature can produce thought; but can I better explain its operation in the formation of a plant or in the motion of an animal? To attempt to deduce thought from any mere combination of matter is a perversity into which I shall not fall; but can I thus explain even the formation of the simplest moss? Those original powers of Nature cannot be explained, for it is only by them that we can explain everything which is susceptible of explanation. Thought exists; its existence is absolute and independent just as the formative power of Nature exists absolutely and independently. It is in Nature; for the thinking being arises and develops himself according to the laws of Nature; therefore thought exists through Nature. There is in Nature an original thinking-power, as there is an original formative-power.

This original thinking-power of the Universe goes forth and develops itself in all possible modes of which it is capable, as the other original forces of Nature go forth and assume all forms possible to them. Like the plant, I am a particular mode or manifestation of the formative-power; like the animal, a particular mode or manifestation of the power of motion; and besides these I am also a particular mode or manifestation of the thinking-power; and the union of these three original powers into one—into one harmonious development—is the distinguishing characteristic of my species, as it is the distinguishing characteristic of the plant species to be merely a mode or manifestation of the formative-power.

Form, motion, and thought, in me, are not dependent on each other or consequent on each other. I cannot be said to think and thereby conceive of the forms and motions that surround me in such or such a manner because they are so; nor, on the other hand, can they be said to be so because I so conceive of them. They are all simultaneous and harmonious developments of one and the same power, the manifestation of which necessarily assumes the form of a complete creature of my species, and which may thus be called the power to form a man. A thought arises within me absolutely, without dependence on anything else; the corresponding form likewise arises absolutely, and also the motion which corresponds to both. I cannot be said to be what I am because I think it or will it; nor can I be said to think and will it because I am so; but I am, and I think, both absolutely; my being and my thinking are in accord by virtue of a higher power.

As surely as those original powers of Nature exist for themselves, and have their own internal laws and purposes, so surely must their outward manifestations, if they are left to themselves and are not suppressed by any foreign force, endure for a certain period of time and describe a certain circle of change. That which disappears even at the moment of its production is assuredly not the manifestation of one primordial power, but only a consequence of the combined operation of various powers. The plant, a particular mode or manifestation of Nature's power of formation, when left to itself, proceeds from the first germination to the ripening of the seed. Man, a particular mode or manifestation of all the powers of Nature in their union, when left to himself, proceeds from birth to death in old age. Hence the duration of the life of plants and of men, and the varied modes of this life.

These essential qualities—this form, this proper motion, and this thought, in harmony with each other—amid many nonessential changes continue to belong to me in so far as I am a member of my species. But Nature's power of producing a human person had already displayed itself before I existed, under a multitude of outward conditions and circumstances. Such outward circumstances have determined the particular manner of its present activity, which has resulted in the production of precisely such an individual of my species as I am. The same circumstances can never return, unless the whole course of Nature should repeat itself and two Natures arise instead of one; hence individuals who have existed can never come into being again. Moreover, Nature's power of forming a human person manifests itself, during the time in which I exist, under all conditions and circumstances possible in that time. But no combination of circumstances can perfectly resemble those through which I came into existence, unless the universe could divide itself into two perfectly similar but independent worlds. It is impossible that two perfectly similar individuals can come into actual existence at the same time. It is thus determined what I, this definite person, must be; and the general law by which I am what I am is discovered. Nature's power of forming a human person having been what it was, being what it is, and standing in this particular relation to the other opposing powers of Nature, I am that which this power *could become;* and— there being no ground of limitation within itself—since it *could* become, necessarily *must become.* I am that which I am, because in the particular position of the great system of Nature only such a person, and absolutely no other, was possible. A spirit who could look through the innermost secrets of Nature would, from knowing one single man, be able distinctly to declare what men had formerly existed, and what men would exist at any future moment; in one individual he would discern *all* individuals. It is this, my interconnection with the whole system of Nature, which determines what I have been, what I am, and what I shall be. From any possible moment of my existence the same spirit could deduce infallibly what I had previously been, and what I was afterwards to become. All that, at any time, I am and shall be, I am and shall be of absolute necessity; and it is impossible that I should be anything else.

I am, indeed, conscious of myself as an independent and, in many occurrences of my life, a free being; but this consciousness may easily be explained on the principles already laid down, and may be thoroughly reconciled with the conclusions which have been drawn. My immediate consciousness, my proper perception, cannot go beyond myself and the modes of my own being. I have immediate knowledge of myself alone: whatever I may know more than this, I know only by inference, in the same way in which I have inferred the existence of original powers of Nature, which yet do not lie within the circle of my perceptions. But I myself—that which I call *me*, my personality —am not the same as Nature's power of producing a human being; I am only one of the manifestations of this power. And in being conscious of myself, I am conscious only of this manifestation and not of that power whose existence I infer when I try to explain my own. This manifestation, however, in its true nature, is really the product of an original and independent power, and must appear as such in consciousness. On this account I recognize myself generally as an independent being. For this reason I appear to myself *as free* in certain occurrences of my life, when these occurrences are the manifestations of the independent power which falls to my share as an individual; *as restrained and limited,* when, by any combination of outward circumstances, which may arise in time, but do not lie within the original limitations of my personality, I cannot do what my individual power would naturally, if unobstructed, be capable of doing; *as compelled,* when this individual power, by the superiority of antagonistic powers, is constrained to manifest itself even in opposition to the laws of its own nature.

Bestow consciousness on a tree, and let it grow, spread out its branches, and bring forth leaves and buds, blossoms and fruits, after its kind, without hindrance or obstruction —it will perceive no limitation to its existence in being only a tree, a tree of this particular species, and this particular individual of the species; it will feel itself perfectly *free,* because, in all those manifestations, it will do nothing but what its nature requires; and it will desire to do nothing else, because it can desire only what that nature requires. But let its growth be hindered by unfavorable weather.

want of nourishment, or other causes, and it will feel itself *limited and restrained,* because an impulse which actually belongs to its nature is not satisfied. Bind its free-waving boughs to a wall, force foreign branches on it by ingrafting, and it will feel itself *compelled* to one course of action; its branches will grow, but not in the direction they would have taken if left to themselves; it will produce fruits, but not those which belong to its original nature. In immediate consciousness, I appear to myself as free; by reflection on the whole of Nature, I discover that freedom is absolutely impossible; the former must be subordinate to the latter, for it can be explained only by means of it.

What high satisfaction is attained through the system which my understanding has thus built up! What order, what firm connection, what comprehensive supervision does it introduce into the whole fabric of my knowledge! Consciousness is here no longer that stranger in Nature whose connection with existence is so incomprehensible; it is native to it, and indeed one of its necessary manifestations. Nature rises gradually in the fixed series of her productions. In rude matter she is a simple existence; in organized matter she returns within herself to internal activity—in the plant, to produce form; in the animal, motion. In man, as her highest masterpiece, she turns inward, that she may perceive and contemplate herself. It is as though Nature reproduces herself in man and, from mere existence, becomes existence and consciousness in one.

In this connection it is easy to understand how I am conscious of my own being and of its determinations. My being and my knowledge have one common foundation—my own nature. The being within me, even because it is my being, is conscious of itself. My consciousness of corporeal objects existing beyond myself is also easy to conceive. The powers in whose manifestation my personality consists—

the formative, the self-moving, the thinking powers—are only a certain portion of these same powers as they exist in Nature at large; this is because of the fact that there are so many other existences beyond me. From the former, I can infer the latter; from the limitation, that which limits. Because I myself am not this or that, which yet belongs to the connected system of existence, it must exist beyond me—thus reasons the thinking principle within me. Of my own limitation I am immediately conscious, because it is part of myself, and only by reason of it do I possess an actual existence. From this consciousness of myself arises my consciousness of the source of this limitation—of that which I myself am not.

My knowledge of external things, then, does not flow from them; their pretended influences and operations cannot bring me a knowledge which is not in themselves. The ground upon which I assume the existence of something beyond myself does not lie outside of myself, but within me, in the limitation of my own personality. By means of this limitation, the thinking principle of Nature within me proceeds outside of itself and is able to survey itself as a whole, although, in each individual, from a different point of view.

In the same way there arises within me the idea of other thinking beings like myself. I, or the thinking power of Nature within me, possess some thoughts which seem to have developed themselves within myself as a particular form of Nature; and others, which seem not to have so developed themselves. And so it is in reality. The former are my own peculiar, individual contributions to the general circle of thought in Nature; the latter are deduced from them, as what must surely have a place in that circle; but being only inferences so far as I am concerned, they must find that place, not in me, but in other thinking beings. Hence I conclude that there are other thinking beings besides myself. In short, Nature becomes in me conscious of herself as a whole, but only by beginning with my own individual consciousness, and proceeding from thence to the consciousness of universal being by inference founded on the principle of causality; that is to say, Nature is conscious of the conditions under which alone such a form, such a motion, such a thought as that in which my personality consists is possible. The principle of causality is the point of transition, from the particular within myself to the universal which lies beyond myself; and the distinguishing characteristic of those two kinds of knowledge is this, that the one is immediate perception, while the other is inference.

In each individual, Nature beholds herself from a particular point of view. I refer to myself as *I* and to you as *you*. You call yourself *I*, and me *you*. I exist beyond you, as you exist beyond me. Of what there is beyond me, I comprehend first those things which touch me most nearly; you, those which touch you most nearly—from these points we each proceed to the next step; but we traverse very different paths, which may here and there intersect each other, but never run parallel. There is an infinite variety of possible individuals, and hence also an infinite variety of possible starting points of consciousness. This consciousness of all individuals, taken together, constitutes the complete consciousness of the universe; and there is no other, for only in the individual is there definite completeness and reality.

The testimony of consciousness in each individual is altogether sure and trustworthy, if it be, indeed, the consciousness here described; for this consciousness develops itself out of the whole prescribed course of Nature, and Nature cannot contradict herself. Wherever there is a conception, there must be something real which corresponds to it; for the production of conceptions must be simultaneous with that of the corresponding realities. To each individual his own particular consciousness is wholly determined, for it proceeds from his own nature; no one can have other conceptions, or a greater or less degree of vitality in these conceptions, than he actually has. The substance of his conceptions is determined by the position which he assumes in the universe; their clearness and vitality, by the higher or lower degree of efficiency manifested by the power of humanity in his person. Let Nature determine a man in a single respect, however trivial—the path of a muscle or the turn of a hair: if Nature had a universal consciousness and could reply to your questions, it could then tell you every thought which could belong to this man during the whole period of his conscious existence.

In this system also, the phenomenon of our consciousness which we call Will becomes thoroughly intelligible. A volition is the immediate consciousness of the activity of any of the powers of Nature within us. The immediate consciousness of an effort of these powers which has not yet become a reality, because it is hemmed in by opposing powers, is, in consciousness, inclination or desire; the struggle of contending powers is irresolution; the victory of one is the determination of the Will. If the power which strives after activity be one we have in common only with the plant or the animal, there arises a division and degradation of our inward being; the desire is unworthy of our rank in the order of things, and, according to a common use of language, may be called a lower desire. If this striving power be the whole undivided force of humanity, then the desire is worthy of our nature and may be called one which is higher. The latter effort, considered absolutely, may be called a moral law. The effect of this latter is a virtuous Will, and the course of action resulting from it is virtue. The triumph of the former not in harmony with the latter is vice; such a triumph *over* the latter, and despite its opposition, is crime.

The power, which on each individual occasion proves triumphant, triumphs of necessity; its superiority is determined by the whole connection of the universe; hence by this connection the vice or crime of each individual is irrevocably determined. Let Nature, once again, determine the path of a muscle, or the turn of a hair, in any particular individual; if Nature had the power of thinking upon the whole and could reply to your questions, it could tell you of all the good and evil deeds of this man's life from the beginning to the end of it. Nevertheless, virtue does not cease to be virtue, nor vice to be vice. The virtuous man is a noble product of Nature; the vicious, an ignoble and contemptible one: yet both are necessary results of the connected system of the universe.

Repentance is the consciousness of the continued effort of humanity within me, even after it has been overcome, associated with the disagreeable sense of having been subdued—a disquieting but still precious pledge of our nobler nature. From this consciousness of the fundamental impulse of our nature arises the sense which has been called "conscience," and its greater or less degree of strictness and susceptibility, down to the absolute want of it in many individuals. The ignoble man is incapable of repentance, for in him humanity has at no time sufficient strength to contend with the lower impulses. Reward and punishment are the natural consequences of virtue and vice for the production of new virtue and new vice. By frequent and important victories, our peculiar power is extended and strengthened; by inaction or frequent defeat, it becomes ever weaker. The ideas of guilt and accountability have no meaning outside of external legislation. Man incurs guilt, and must render an account of his crime only if he compels society to use artificial, external force to restrain those of his impulses which are injurious to the general welfare.

My inquiry is closed, and my desire of knowledge satisfied. I know what I am, and wherein the nature of my species consists. I am a manifestation, determined by the whole system of the universe, of a power of Nature which is deter-mined by itself alone. To know my particular personal being by knowing its deepest sources is impossible, for I cannot penetrate into the innermost recesses of Nature. But I am *immediately* conscious of my personal existence. I know right well what I am at the present moment; I can for the most part remember what I have been formerly; and I shall learn what I shall be when what is now future shall become present experience.

Yet I cannot make use of this discovery in the regulation of my actions, for I do not truly act at all: Nature acts in me. To make myself anything other than that which Nature has intended is something I cannot even propose to myself. I am not the author of my own being; Nature has made me what I am and everything that I am going to be. I may repent and rejoice and form good resolutions—although, strictly speaking, I cannot even do this, for all these things come to me of themselves when it is appointed for them to come. But it is certain that, with all my repentance and all my resolutions, I cannot produce the smallest change in that which I must inevitably become. I stand under the inexorable power of rigid necessity: if this necessity has destined me to become a fool and a profligate, a fool and a profligate without doubt I shall become; if it has destined me to be wise and good, wise and good I shall doubtless be. Blame and merit do not apply to necessity, nor do they apply to me. Necessity stands under its own laws. I stand under them as well. I see this and feel that my tranquillity would be best ensured if I could make my wishes accord with that necessity to which my being is wholly subject.

But, oh, these conflicting wishes! For why should I any longer hide from myself the sadness, the horror, the amaze-ment with which I was filled when I saw how my inquiry must end? I had solemnly promised myself that my inclinations should have no influence in the direction of my thoughts; and I have not knowingly allowed them any such influence. But now, at the end, may I not confess that this result contradicts the profoundest aspirations, wishes, and wants of my being? And, despite the accuracy and the decisive strictness of proofs, how can I truly believe in a theory of my being which strikes at the very root of that being, which so distinctly contradicts all the purposes for which alone I live, and without which I should loathe my existence?

Why must my heart grieve over, and be torn by, that which so perfectly satisfies my understanding? Since nothing in Nature contradicts itself, is man alone a contradiction? Or perhaps not man in general, but only myself and those who resemble me? Had I but remained amid the pleasant delusions that surrounded me, satisfied with the immediate consciousness of my existence, and had never raised those questions concerning its foundation! But if the answer—which has caused me this misery—be true, then I *must* of necessity have raised these questions: or, rather, the thinking nature within me—and not I myself—raised them. I was destined to this misery, and it is in vain that I mourn the lost innocence of soul which can never return.

But courage! Let all else be lost, so that this at least remains! Merely for the sake of my wishes, however profound they may be and however sacred they may seem, I cannot renounce what rests on incontrovertible evidence. But perhaps I may have erred in my investigation; perhaps I may have only partially comprehended and imperfectly considered the grounds upon which I had to proceed. I ought to retrace the inquiry again from the opposite end, in order that I may at least possess a correct starting point What is it, then, that I find so repugnant, so painful, in the decision to which I have come? What is it which I desired to find in its place? Let me before all things make clear to myself what are these inclinations to which I appeal.

That I should be destined to be wise and good, or to be foolish and profligate, without power to change this destiny in the least—in the former case having no merit, and in the latter having no guilt: this it was that filled me with amazement and horror. That my very being and all of its characteristics should be determined by something external to me,[1] and that this thing in turn should be determined by something external to it: it was this from which I so violently recoiled. That whatever freedom there may be in the world be freedom which is not my own but that of some power other than myself—and even then only a limited half-freedom: it was this which did not satisfy me. What I had desired was this: that I myself, that of which I am conscious as my own being and person, but which in this system appears as only the manifestation of a higher existence, that this "I" would be independent, would be something which exists not by another or through another, but of myself, and, as such, would be the final root of all my own determinations. The rank which in this system is assumed by an original power of Nature I would myself assume; with this difference, that my nature would not be determined by any foreign power. I desire to possess an inward and peculiar power of manifestation, infinitely manifold like those powers of Nature; and this power shall manifest itself in the particular way in which it does manifest itself, for no other reason than because it does so manifest itself; not, like these powers of Nature, because it is placed under such or such outward conditions.

What then, according to my wish, shall be the especial seat and center of this peculiar inward power? Evidently not my body, for that I willingly allow to pass for a manifestation of the powers of Nature—at least in its existence,

[1] [The phrase *"ausser mir"* has been translated throughout as "external to me."]

if not with regard to its further determinations; not my sensuous inclinations, for these I regard as a relation of those powers to my consciousness. Hence it must be my thought and will. I would exercise my voluntary power freely, for the accomplishment of aims which I shall have freely adopted; and this will, as its ultimate ground can be determined by no higher, shall move and mold, first my own body, and through it the surrounding world. My active powers shall be under the control of my will alone, and shall be set in motion by nothing else than by it. Thus it shall be. There shall be a Supreme Good in the spiritual world; I shall have the power to seek this with freedom until I find it, to acknowledge it as such when found, and it shall be my fault if I do not find it. This Supreme Good I shall will to know, merely because I will it; and if I will anything else instead of it, the fault shall be mine. My actions shall be the result of this will; without it I shall not act at all, since there shall be no other power over my actions but this will. Then my powers, determined by and subject to the dominion of, my will, will affect the external world. I will be the lord of Nature, and she shall be my servant. I will influence her according to the measure of my capacity, but she shall have no influence on me.

This, then, is the substance of my wishes and aspirations. But the system, which has satisfied my understanding, has wholly repudiated these. According to the one, I am wholly independent of Nature and of any law which I do not impose upon myself; according to the other, I am but a strictly determined link in the chain of Nature. Whether such a freedom as I have desired be at all conceivable, and, if so, whether a complete and thorough investigation would reveal grounds compelling me to accept this freedom as a reality and to ascribe it to myself, thereby refuting my former conclusions—this is now the question.

To be free, in the sense stated, means that I myself will make myself whatever I am to be. I must, then—and this is what is most surprising and, at first sight, absurd in the idea—I must already be, in a certain sense, that which I shall become, in order to be able to become so; I must possess a two-fold being, of which the first shall contain the determining ground of the second. If I observe my immediate self-consciousness on this matter, I find the following: I have the knowledge of various possible courses of action, from amongst which, as it appears to me, I may choose which I please. I run through the whole circle, enlarge it, examine the various courses, compare one with another, and consider. Finally I decide upon one, determine my will in accordance with it, and this resolution of my will is followed by a corresponding action. In the mere conception of a purpose I am already that which I subsequently become once I have willed and acted upon this purpose. I am beforehand as a *thinking* what I am afterwards as an *active* being. I create myself: my being by my thought, my thought by thought itself. In the case of something which manifests a mere power of nature, a plant, for instance, one can conceive a determinate state as preceded by an indeterminate state which provides the theory with an infinite variety of possible determinations. These manifold possibilities are certainly possibilities *within it,* contained in its original constitution, but they are not possibilities *for it,* because it is incapable of having an idea and cannot choose, or of itself put, an end to this indeterminate state. There must be external grounds by which it may be determined to some one of those various possibilities to which it is unable to determine itself. This determination can have no previous existence within it, for it is capable of but one mode of determination—that which it has actually assumed. Hence it was that I formerly felt myself compelled to maintain that the manifestation of every power must receive its final determination from without. Doubtless, I then thought only of such powers as are incapable of consciousness and manifest themselves merely in the outward world.

To them that assertion may be applied without the slightest limitation; but to intelligences the grounds of it are not applicable, and it was, therefore, rash to extend it to them.

Freedom, such as I have laid claim to, is conceivable only of intelligences; but to them, undoubtedly, it belongs. Under this supposition, man, as well as nature, is perfectly comprehensible. My body and my capacity of operating in the world of sense are, as in the former system, manifestations of certain limited powers of Nature; and my natural inclinations are the relations of these manifestations to my consciousness. The mere knowledge of what exists independently of me arises under this supposition of freedom, precisely as in the former system; and up to this point, both agree. But according to the former—and here begins the opposition between these systems—according to the former, my capacity of physical activity remains under the dominion of Nature and is constantly set in motion by the same power which produced it, and thought has here nothing whatever to do but to look on. According to the latter, this capacity of physical activity, once brought into existence, falls under the dominion of a power superior to Nature and wholly independent of her laws—the power of determinate purpose and of will. Thought is no longer the mere faculty of observation; it is the source of action itself. In the one case, my state of indecision is resolved by forces, external and invisible to me, which limit my activity as well as my immediate consciousness of it—that is, my will—to a single course; this is the way in which the indeterminate state of the plant is resolved. But in the other case it is I myself, independent and free from the influence of all outward forces, who put an end to my state of indecision and determine my own course according to the knowledge I have freely attained of what is best.

Which of these two opinions shall I adopt? Am I free and independent or am I nothing in myself, and merely the manifestation of a foreign power? It is clear to me that neither of the two doctrines is sufficiently supported. For the first, there is no other recommendation than the mere fact that it is conceivable; for the latter, I extend a principle which is perfectly true in its own place, beyond its proper and natural application. If intelligence is merely the manifestation of a power of Nature, then I do quite right to extend this principle to it; but the very question at issue is whether intelligence is such a manifestation. And this is a question which is not to be answered by deducing a one-sided assumption which I have made at the start of my inquiry; the question must be answered by reference to other premises. In short, it would seem that neither of the two opinions can be established by appeal to proofs.

Nor can the question be settled by immediate consciousness. I can never become conscious of the external powers by which, in the system of universal necessity, I am determined; nor can I become conscious of my own power by which, on the system of freedom, I determine myself. Thus, whichever of the two opinions I may accept, I accept it merely by arbitrary choice.

The system of freedom satisfies my heart; the opposite system destroys and annihilates it. To stand, cold and unmoved, amid the current of events, a passive mirror of fugitive and passing phenomena—this existence is insupportable to me; I scorn and detest it. I will love; I will lose myself in sympathy; I will know the joy and the grief of life. I myself am the highest object of this sympathy; and the only way in which I can justify its requirements is by my actions. I will do all for the best—I will rejoice when I have done right, I will grieve when I have done wrong; and even this sorrow shall be sweet to me, for it is a chord of sympathy, a pledge of future amendment. In love only there is life; without it is death and annihilation.

But the opposite system advances coldly and insolently, turning this love into a mockery. If I listen to it, I no longer exist and I cannot act. The object of my most intimate attachment is a phantom of the brain—a gross and palpable delusion. I do not act; a foreign power, wholly unknown, acts within me; and it is a matter of indifference to me how this power unfolds itself. I stand abashed, with my warm affections and my virtuous will, and blush for what I know to be best and purest in my nature, for the sake of which alone I would exist, as for a ridiculous folly. What is holiest in me is given over as a prey to scorn.

Doubtless it was the love of this love, an interest in this interest which, at the outset of this perplexing and distracting inquiry, unconsciously led me to regard myself as free and independent; doubtless it was this interest which has led me to an opinion having nothing in its favor but its intelligibility and the impossibility of proving its opposite. It was this interest which has hitherto restrained me from seeking any further explanation of myself and my capacities.

The opposite system, barren and heartless indeed, but exhaustless in its explanations, will explain even this desire for freedom and this aversion to the contrary doctrine. It explains everything which I can cite from my own consciousness against it, and as often as I say "thus and thus is the case," it replies with the same cool complacency, "I say so, too; and I tell you besides why it must *necessarily* be so." It will answer all my complaints in this way: "When you speak of your heart, your love, and your interest, you speak from the standpoint of your own immediate self-consciousness; you have already confessed this in asserting that you are yourself the object of your highest interest. Now it is already well known, and we proved it above, that this you, for whom you are so deeply interested, in so far as it is not the mere activity of your individual inward nature, is at least an impulse of it. Every such impulse, as surely as it exists, returns on itself and impels itself to activity. We can thus understand how this impulse must manifest itself in consciousness, as love for, and interest in, free

individual activity. If you could exchange the narrow point
of view of self-consciousness for the higher perspective from
which you may grasp the universe, a perspective which indeed you have promised yourself to take, then it would
become clear that what you have called your love is not
your love, but a foreign love—the interest which the original
power of Nature, manifesting itself in you, takes in main-
taining its own peculiar existence. Do not then appeal again
to your love; for even if that could prove anything, its
supposition here is wholly irregular and unjustifiable. *You*
do not love yourself, for, strictly speaking, there is no you;
it is Nature within you which concerns itself with its own
preservation. You have admitted without dispute that, although in the plant there exists a peculiar impulse to grow
and develop itself, the specific activity of this impulse depends upon forces lying beyond itself. If the plant could
be made conscious, then it would regard this instinct of
growth with interest and love. And if it could be persuaded that this instinct cannot itself accomplish anything
and that the measure of its manifestation is always determined by something beyond itself—then it would speak
just as you have spoken. It would behave in a manner that
may be pardoned in a plant, but which is hardly fitting for
you—a higher product of Nature which is capable of understanding the universe."

What reply can I make? If I were to adopt this celebrated
point of view, from which I could grasp the entire universe,
then doubtless I would be forced to blush and be silent.
This, therefore, is the question: whether I shall at once
assume this position or whether I shall confine myself to
the range of immediate self-consciousness; whether love
shall be made subject to knowledge or knowledge to love.
The latter stands in bad esteem among intelligent people;
the former renders me indescribably miserable, by extin-
guishing my own personal being within me. I cannot do
the latter without appearing inconsiderate and foolish in

my own estimation; I cannot do the former without deliberately annihilating my own existence.

I cannot remain in this state of indecision; on the solution of this question depends my whole peace and dignity. And it is impossible for me to reach a decision. I have absolutely no ground for making a decision in favor of the one opinion or the other.

This is an intolerable state of uncertainty and irresolution. Through the best and most courageous resolution of my life, I have been reduced to this! What power can deliver me from it? What power can deliver me from myself?

BOOK TWO

KNOWLEDGE

Chagrin and anguish stung me to the heart. I cursed the returning day which called me back to an existence whose truth and significance were now involved in doubt. I awoke in the night from unquiet dreams. I sought anxiously for a ray of light that might lead me out of these mazes of uncertainty. I sought, but became only more deeply entangled in the labyrinth.

Once, at the hour of midnight, a wondrous shape appeared before me, and addressed me:—

"Poor mortal," I heard it say, "you heap error upon error, and fancy yourself wise. You tremble before the phantoms which you yourself have toiled to create. Have the courage to become truly wise. I bring you no new revelation. What I can teach you, you already know; you have only to recall it. I cannot deceive you; for in every step you will acknowledge me to be in the right; and should you still be deceived, you will be deceived by yourself. Take courage; listen to me, and answer my questions."

I took courage. "He appeals to my own understanding. I will make the venture. He cannot think his own thoughts into my mind; the conclusion to which I shall come must be thought out by myself; the conviction which I shall accept must be of my own creating. Speak, wonderful Spirit!" I exclaimed, "whatever you are! Speak, and I will listen. Question me, and I will answer."

The Spirit. You believe that these objects here, and those there, are actually present before you and outside of yourself?

I. Certainly I do.

35

Spirit. And how do you know they are actually present?

I. I see them; I would feel them if I were to stretch forth my hand; I can hear the sounds they produce; they reveal themselves to me through all my senses.

Spirit. Indeed! Later you may take back the assertion that you see, feel, and hear these objects. For the present I will speak as you do, as if, by means of your sight, touch, and hearing, you really do perceive the real existence of objects. But observe: it is only *by means of* your sight, touch, and other external senses. Or is it not so? Do you perceive otherwise than through your senses? Is an object in any way present to you other than as you see it or feel it, etc.?

I. By no means.

Spirit. Sensible objects, therefore, exist for you only in consequence of a particular determination of your external senses: you know of them only as a result of your knowledge of this determination of your sight, touch, etc. Your assertion, "these are objects external to me," depends upon this other—"I see, hear, feel, and so forth?"

I. That is my meaning.

Spirit. And how do you know that you see, hear, and feel?

I. I do not understand you. Your questions appear strange to me.

Spirit. I will make them more intelligible. Do you see your sight, and feel your touch, or have you a still higher sense through which you perceive your external senses and their determinations?

I. By no means. I know immediately *that* I see and feel, and I know immediately *what* it is that I see and feel; I know this while it is, and simply because it is, without the intervention of any other sense. That is why your question seemed strange to me, because it appeared to throw doubt on this immediate consciousness.

Spirit. That was not my intention. I wanted you to make this immediate consciousness clear to yourself. You have, then, an immediate consciousness of your sight and touch?

I. Yes.

Spirit. Of your sight and touch, I said. Hence you are that which sees and which feels; and when you are conscious of the seeing, feeling, etc., you are conscious of a particular determination or modification of *yourself.*

I. Unquestionably.

Spirit. You have a consciousness of your seeing, feeling, etc., and thereby you perceive the object. Could you not perceive it without this consciousness? Can you not recognize an object by sight or hearing, without knowing that you see or hear?

I. By no means.

Spirit. The immediate consciousness of yourself, and of your own determinations, is therefore the imperative condition of all other consciousness; and you know a thing only in so far as you know that you know it; no element can enter into the latter cognition which is not contained in the former. You cannot know anything without knowing that you know it?

I. I think not.

Spirit. Therefore, you know of the existence of objects only by means of seeing, feeling them, etc., and you know that you see and feel only by means of an immediate consciousness of this knowledge. What you do not perceive *immediately,* you do not perceive at all.

I. I see that that is so.

Spirit. In all perception, you perceive in the first place only yourself and your own condition; whatever is not contained in this perception is not perceived at all?

I. You repeat what I have already admitted.

Spirit. I would not weary of repeating it in all its applications if I thought that you had not thoroughly comprehended it and indelibly impressed it on your mind. Can you say: I am conscious of external objects?

I. By no means, if I speak accurately; for the sight and

touch by which I grasp these objects are not consciousness itself, but only that of which I am first and most immediately conscious. Strictly speaking, I can say only that I am conscious of my seeing and touching of these objects.

Spirit. Do not forget, then, what you have now clearly understood. *In all perception you perceive only your own condition.*

Spirit. I shall, however, continue to speak your language, since it is most familiar to you. You have said that you can see, hear, and feel objects. How then—that is, with what properties or attributes—do you see or feel them?

I. I see that that object is red, this blue; when I touch them, I find this smooth, that rough—this cold, that warm.

Spirit. You know then what red, blue, smooth, rough, cold, and warm, really are?

I. Undoubtedly I do.

Spirit. Will you not describe them to me then?

I. They cannot be described. Look! Turn your eye toward that object: what you become conscious of through your sight, I call red. Touch the surface of this other object: what you feel, I call smooth. In this way I have arrived at this knowledge, and there is no other way by which it can be acquired.

Spirit. But can we not, at least from some of these qualities known by immediate sensation, deduce a knowledge of others differing from them? If, for instance, anyone had seen red, green, yellow, but never a blue color, had tasted sour, sweet, salt, but never bitter, could he not discover, by mere reflection and comparison, what blue is, or what bitter is, without having ever seen or tasted anything of the kind?

I. Certainly not. What is a matter of sensation can only be experienced, it is not discoverable by thought; it is no deduction, but a direct and immediate perception.

Spirit. Strange! You boast of a knowledge, but you cannot tell me how you have attained it. For, see, you maintain that you can see one quality in an object, feel another, hear a third; you must, therefore, be able to distinguish sight from touch, and both from hearing?

I. Without doubt.

Spirit. You maintain further that you see this object to be red, that to be blue; and feel this as smooth, and that as rough. You must therefore be able to distinguish red from blue, smooth from rough?

I. Without doubt.

Spirit. And you maintain that you have not discovered this difference by means of reflection and comparison of these sensations in yourself. But perhaps you have learned, by comparing the red or blue colors, the smooth or rough surfaces of *objects external to yourself,* what you should experience *within yourself* as red or blue, smooth or rough?

I. This is impossible; for my perception of objects proceeds from my perception of my own internal condition, and is determined by it—not the reverse. I first distinguish objects by distinguishing my own states of being. I can learn that this particular sensation is indicated by the arbitrary sign, red; and those by the signs, blue, smooth, rough; but I cannot learn that the sensations themselves are distinguished, nor how they are distinguished. *That* they are different, I know only by being conscious of my own feelings, and that I feel differently regarding them. *How* they differ, I cannot describe, but I know that they must differ just as my feeling regarding them differs; and this difference of feeling is an immediate, and by no means an acquired or inferred, distinction.

Spirit. A distinction which you can make independently of all knowledge of the objects themselves?

I. Which I *must* make independently of such knowledge, for this knowledge is itself dependent on that distinction.

Spirit. Which is then given to you immediately through mere self-consciousness?

I. In no other way.

Spirit. But then you should content yourself with saying, "I feel myself affected in the manner that I call red, blue, smooth, rough." You should refer these sensations to yourself alone and not transfer them to an external object. You should not attribute to an external object what is really a property of yourself.

Or, tell me: when you think you see that an object is red, or feel that it is smooth, do you really perceive anything more than that you are affected in a certain manner?

I. From what has gone before, I clearly see that I do not, in fact, perceive more than what you say; and this transference of what is in me to something external to me, though it is something from which I cannot refrain, now appears very strange to me.

My sensations are in myself, not in the object, for I am myself and not the object; I am conscious only of myself and of my own state, not of the state of the object. If there is a consciousness of the object, that consciousness is, certainly, neither sensation nor perception—so much is clear.

Spirit. You form your conclusions somewhat precipitately. Let us consider this matter on all sides, so that I may be assured that you will not again retract what you have now freely admitted.

As you usually think of the object, is there anything more to it than its red color, its smooth surface, and so on—in short, anything other than those characteristic marks which you obtain through immediate sensation?

I. I believe that there is; in addition to these attributes there is the thing itself to which they belong; that which bears these attributes.

Spirit. But through what sense do you perceive this bearer of attributes? Do you see it, feel it, hear it? Or is there perhaps a special sense for its perception?

I. No. I think that I see and feel it.

Spirit. Indeed! Let us examine this more closely. Are you ever conscious of your sight in itself, or are you conscious only of determinate acts of sight?

I. I am conscious always of a determinate sensation of sight.

Spirit. And what is this determinate sensation of sight with respect to that object there?

I. That of red color.

Spirit. And this red is something positive, a simple sensation, a specific state of yourself?

I. This is what I now can understand.

Spirit. You should, therefore, see the red in itself as simple, as a mathematical point, and see it only as such. In you at least, as an affection of you, it is obviously a simple, determinate state, without connection with anything else—something we can describe only as a mathematical point. Or do you find it otherwise?

I. I must admit that it is as you say.

Spirit. But now you spread this simple red over a broad surface, which you assuredly *do not see,* since you see only the red. How do you arrive at this surface?

I. It is certainly strange. Yet I believe that I have found the explanation. I do not, indeed, see the surface, but I *feel* it when I pass my hand over it. My sensation of sight remains the same during this process of feeling, and hence I extend the red color over the whole surface which I *feel* while I continue to *see* the same red.

Spirit. This might be so, if you really did feel the surface. But let us see whether that is possible. You do not feel absolutely; you feel only your feelings, and are only conscious of these?

I. By no means. Each sensation is a determinate something. I never merely see or hear or feel in general, but my sensations are always definite. Red, green, blue colors, cold, warmth, smoothness, roughness, the sound of the violin, the voice of man, and the like; these are what I see, feel, or hear. Let that be settled between us.

Spirit. Willingly. Thus, when you said that you felt a surface, you had only an immediate consciousness of feeling smooth, rough, or the like?

I. Certainly.

Spirit. This smooth or rough is, like the red color, a simple sensation—a point within yourself, the one who is having the experience? And with the same right with which I formerly asked why you spread a simple sensation of sight over an imaginary surface, I now ask why you should do the same with a simple sensation of touch?

I. This smooth surface is perhaps not equally smooth in all points, but has in each a different degree of smoothness. I am not able to distinguish these degrees from each other with any strictness and I do not have words with which I can retain and express their differences. Yet I do distinguish them, unconsciously, and place them side by side; and thus I form the conception of a surface.

Spirit. But can you, in the same undivided moment of time, have sensations of opposite kinds or be affected at the same time in different ways?

I. By no means.

Spirit. Those different degrees of smoothness, which you would assume in order to explain what you cannot explain, are therefore, in so far as they are different from each other, mere opposite sensations which succeed each other in you?

I. I cannot deny this.

Spirit. You should therefore describe them as you really find them—as successive changes of the same mathematical point, such as you perceive in other cases; you should not describe them as adjacent and simultaneous qualities of several points in one surface.

I. I see this, and I find that nothing is explained by my assumption. But my hand, with which I touch the object and cover it, is itself a surface; and by means of my hand

I perceive the object to be a surface, and a greater one than my hand, since I can extend my hand several times upon it.

Spirit. Your hand is a surface? How do you know that? How do you attain any consciousness of your hand at all? Do you feel it or do you feel itself by means of some other part of your body, in which case it is an object? Or is there some other way of becoming conscious of it?

I. No, there is no other. With my hand I feel some other definite object, or I feel my hand itself by means of some other part of my body. I have no immediate, absolute consciousness of my hand, any more than of my sight or touch.

Spirit. Let us, at present, consider only the case in which your hand is an instrument, for this will determine the second case also. In this case there can be nothing more in the immediate perception than what belongs to sensation—wherein the subject, and in this particular case your hand, is thought of as *that which* touches and feels in the acts of touching and feeling. Now, either your sensation is single or it is varied. But if it is single, then I cannot see why you should extend this single sensation over a sentient surface instead of contenting yourself with a single sentient point. If your sensation is varied, then, since the differences must succeed each other, I again do not see why you should not conceive of these feelings as succeeding each other in one and the same point. That your hand should appear to you as a surface is just as inexplicable as your notion of an external surface in general. Do not make use of the first in order to explain the second until you have explained the first itself. The second case, in which your hand—or whatever other member of your body you choose—is itself the object of a sensation, may easily be explained by means of the first. You perceive this member by means of another, which is then the sentient one. I ask the same questions concerning this latter member that I asked concerning your hand, and you are as little able to answer them as before.

So it is with the surface of your eyes, and with every other surface of your body. It may well be that the consciousness of an extension outside yourself proceeds from the consciousness of your own extension as a material body and is conditioned by it. But then you must, in the first place, explain this extension of your material body.

I. It is enough. I now perceive clearly that I neither see nor feel the superficial extension of the properties of bodies, nor apprehend it by any other sense. I see that it is my habitual practice to extend over a surface what nevertheless in sensation is but one point, to represent as adjacent and simultaneous what I ought to represent as only successive, since in mere sensation there is nothing simultaneous but all is successive. I discover that I proceed in fact exactly as the geometer does in the construction of his figures, extending points to lines and lines to surfaces. I am astonished how I should have done this.

Spirit. You do more than this, and what is even more remarkable: this surface which you attribute to bodies is something which you can neither see nor feel, nor perceive in any other way; but one might say, in a certain sense, that you can see the red color, or feel the smoothness, *upon* this surface. But you add something even to this surface: extend it to a solid mathematical figure, as by your previous admission you extended the line to a surface. You assume a substantial interior existence of the body behind its surface. Tell me, can you then see, feel, or recognize by any sense the actual presence of anything behind this surface?

I. By no means: the space behind the surface is not accessible to my sight, touch, or to any of my senses.

Spirit. And yet you assume the existence of such an interior thing which you plainly do not perceive?

I. I confess it, and my astonishment increases.

Spirit. What then is this something which you imagine to be behind the surface?

I. Well—I suppose something similar to the surface, something tangible.

Spirit. We must be sure of this. Can you divide the mass of which you believe the body to consist?

I. I can divide it to infinity; I do not mean with instruments, but in thought. There is no possible part which is the smallest, which cannot be again divided.

Spirit. And in this division do you ever arrive at a part which you can suppose to be in itself no longer perceptible to sight, touch, and the like; *in itself* I say, besides being imperceptible to your own particular organs of sense?

I. By no means.

Spirit. Visible, perceptible absolutely?—or with certain properties of color, smoothness, roughness, and the like?

I. In the latter way. Nothing is visible or perceptible absolutely, because there is no absolute sense of sight or touch.

Spirit. Then you spread through the whole mass your own sensibility, that which is already familiar to you—visibility as colored, tangibility as rough, smooth, or the like? And it is only this sensibility itself of which you are conscious? Or do you find it otherwise?

I. By no means; what you say follows from what I have already understood and admitted.

Spirit. And yet you perceive nothing behind the surface, and you have perceived nothing there?

I. If I were to break through it, I should perceive something.

Spirit. This is something which you must know beforehand. And the infinite division, in which, as you maintain, you can never arrive at anything absolutely imperceptible, you have never carried it out, nor can you do so?

I. I cannot carry it out.

Spirit. To a sensation, therefore, which you have really had, you add another, in imagination, which you have not had?

I. I am sensible only of that which I attribute to the surface; I am not sensible of what lies behind it, and yet I assume the existence of something there which might be perceived. Yes, I must admit what you say.

Spirit. And the actual sensation is in part found to correspond with what you have thus presupposed?

I. When I break through the surface of a body, I do indeed find beneath it something perceptible, as I presupposed. Yes, I must admit this also.

Spirit. But you have said in part that there is something beyond sensation, which cannot become apparent to any *actual* perception.

I. I maintain that were I to divide a corporeal mass to infinity, I could never come to any part which is *in itself* imperceptible. I admit that I never can carry out the division of a corporeal mass to infinity. Yes, I must also agree with you in this.

Spirit. Thus there is nothing remaining of the object but *what is perceptible,* what is a property or attribute. This perceptibility you extend through a continuous space which is divisible to infinity; and the true bearer of the attributes of things, which you have sought, is, therefore, only the space which is thus filled?

I. Although I cannot be satisfied with this, but feel that I must still suppose in the object something more than this perceptibility and the space it fills, yet I cannot point out this something, and I must therefore confess that up to now I have been unable to discover any bearer of attributes other than space itself.

Spirit. Confess always what you see to be true. The present obscurities will gradually become clear, and the unknown will be made known. Space itself, however, is not perceived; and you cannot understand how you have obtained this conception, or why you attribute to it this property of perceptibility?

I. It is so.

Spirit. Nor can you understand how you have obtained

this conception of perceptibility outside of yourself, since you really perceive only your own sensation in yourself, and you perceive it, not as a property of an external thing, but as an affection of your own being.

I. So it is. I see clearly that I really perceive only my own state, and not the object; that I neither see, feel, nor hear this object; but that, on the contrary, precisely there where the object should be, all seeing, feeling, and so forth, comes to an end.

But I have a conjecture. Sensations, as *affections of myself,* have no extension whatever, but are simple states; in their differences they are not contiguous to each other in space, but successive to each other in time. Nevertheless, I do extend them in space. May it not be by means of this extension, and simultaneously with it, that what is properly only my own feeling or sensation becomes changed for me into a perceptible something external to me; and may not this be the precise point at which there arises within me a consciousness of the external object?

Spirit. This conjecture may be confirmed. But could we raise it immediately to a conviction, we should thereby attain to no complete insight, for this higher question would still remain to be answered: How do you, first, come to extend sensation through space? Let us, then, proceed at once to this question, and let us propound it more generally—I have reasons for doing so—in the following manner: How is it that, with your consciousness, which is but an immediate consciousness of yourself, you can proceed beyond yourself and, to the sensation which you perceive, superadd an object, perceived and perceptible, which in fact you do not perceive?

I. Sweet or bitter, fragrant or ill-scented, rough or smooth, cold or warm—these qualities, when applied to things, signify whatever excites in me this or that taste, smell, or other sensation. It is the same with respect to sounds. A relation to myself is always indicated, and it never occurs to me that the sweet or bitter taste, the pleasant or unpleasant smell, lies in the thing itself; it lies in me, and it appears only to be excited by the object. It seems indeed to be otherwise with the sensations of sight—with colors, for example, which may not be pure sensations but a sort of intermediate affection. Yet when we consider it strictly, red and the others mean nothing more than what produces in me certain sensations of sight. This leads me to understand how it is that I attain to a knowledge of things external to me. I am affected in a particular manner—this I know absolutely; this affection must have a foundation; this foundation is not in myself, and therefore must be external to me. Thus I reason rapidly and unconsciously, and forthwith posit such a foundation—namely, *the object*. This foundation must be one by which the particular affection in question may be explained; I am affected in the manner which I call a sweet taste, the object must therefore be of a kind to excite a sweet taste, or, to use an abbreviated manner of speaking, the object must itself be sweet. In this way I arrive at the determination of the object.

Spirit. There may be some truth in what you say, although it is not the whole truth on the subject. How this stands we shall undoubtedly discover in due time. But since it cannot be denied that in other cases you do discover some truth by means of this principle of causality—so I term the doctrine you have just asserted, that everything (in this case your affection) must have a foundation or cause—since this, I say, cannot be denied, we should try to understand this procedure and make it perfectly clear what it is you do when you apply this principle. Let us suppose, for the time being, that your statement is perfectly correct, that it is by an unconscious act of reasoning, from the effect to the cause, that you first come to assume the existence of an external thing. What was it, then, which you were conscious of perceiving?

I. That I was affected in a certain manner.

Spirit. But you were not conscious of an object, affecting you in a certain manner, at least not as a perception?

I. By no means. I have already admitted this.

Spirit. Then, by means of this principle of causality, you add to a knowledge which you have another which you have not?

I. Your words are strange.

Spirit. Perhaps I may succeed in removing this strangeness. But let my words appear to you as they may. They ought only to lead you to produce in your mind the same thought that I have produced in mine; not serve as a textbook which you have only to repeat. When you have the thought itself firmly and clearly in your grasp, then express it as you will, and with as much variety as you will, and be sure that you will always express it well. How, and by what means, do you know of this affection of yourself?

I. It will be difficult to put my answer in words: because my consciousness, as subjective, as a determination of myself in so far as I am an intelligence, proceeds directly upon the existence of this affection as its object, as that of which I am conscious, and is inseparable from it; because I am conscious only to the extent that I know of such an affection—know it absolutely, just as I know of my own existence.

Spirit. You have therefore a means—consciousness itself—whereby you perceive such an affection of yourself?

I. Yes.

Spirit. But you do *not* have any such way of perceiving the object?

I. Since you have convinced me that I neither see nor feel the object itself, nor apprehend it by any external sense, I find myself compelled to confess that I have no such means.

Spirit. Consider this well. This admission may be turned against you. What then *is* your external sense, and how can you call it external, if it has no reference to any external object, and if it is not the means whereby you have any knowledge of such object?

I. I wish to know the truth and I am not concerned about what may be turned against me. I distinguish absolutely green, sweet, red, smooth, bitter, fragrant, rough, ill-scented, the sound of a violin and of a trumpet. Among these sensations I place some in a certain relation of likeness to each other, although in other respects I distinguish them from each other; thus I find green and red, sweet and bitter, rough and smooth, etc., to have a certain relation of similarity to each other, and this similarity I feel to be respectively one of sight, taste, touch, etc. Sight, taste, and so forth, are not indeed in themselves actual sensations, for I never see or feel absolutely, as you have previously remarked, but always see red or green, taste sweet or bitter, etc. Sight, taste, and the like, are not higher determinations of actual sensations; they are classes to which I refer these latter, not by arbitrary arrangement, but guided by the immediate sensation itself. I see in them therefore not external senses, but only particular determinations of the objects of the inner sense, of my own states or affections. How they become external senses, or, more strictly speaking, how I come to regard them as such, and so to name them, is now the question. I do not take back my admission that I have no means of receiving the object itself.

Spirit. Yet you speak of objects as if you really knew of their existence and had a means of acquiring such knowledge?

I. Yes.

Spirit. And you do this, according to your previous assumption, in consequence of the knowledge you really possess, and for which you have an organ of knowing, and you do so on account of this knowledge?

I. That is true.

Spirit. Your real knowledge, that of your sensations or affections, is to you like an imperfect knowledge, which, as you say, requires to be completed by another. This other new knowledge you conceive and describe to yourself—not as something which you have, for you do not have it—but as something which you should have, over and above your actual knowledge, if you had an organ wherewith to apprehend it. "I know nothing indeed," you seem to say, "of things in themselves, but such things there must be; they are to be found, if I could but find them." You suppose another organ, which indeed you do not have, and you apply this to them and thereby apprehend them—of course, in thought only. Strictly speaking, you have no *consciousness of things,* but only *a consciousness* (produced by a passage from your actual consciousness by means of the principle of causality) *of a consciousness of things* (such as ought to be, such as of necessity must be, although not accessible to you); and now you will see that, in the supposition you have made, you have added to a knowledge which you have another which you have not.

I. I must admit this.

Spirit. From now on let us call this second knowledge, obtained by means of another, *mediate,* and the first, *immediate* knowledge. A certain school has called this procedure which we have to some extent described above "a synthesis," by which we are to understand, in this case at least, not a *con-nection* established between two elements previously existing, but an *an-nection,* and an addition of a wholly new element arising through this *an-nection* to another element which had existed independently of such addition.

Thus the *first* consciousness appears as soon as you discover your own existence, and the latter is not discovered without the former; the *second* consciousness is produced in you by means of the first.

I. But not successive to it in time; for I am conscious of external things at the same undivided moment in which I become conscious of myself.

Spirit. I did not speak of such a succession in time at all; but I think that, when you reflect upon that undivided consciousness of yours and of the external object, distinguish between them, and inquire into their connection, you will find that the latter can be conceived of only as conditioned by the former, and as only possible on the supposition of its existence; but not *vice versa*.

I. So I find it to be; and if that be all you would say, I admit your assertion and have already admitted it.

Spirit. You create, I say, this second consciousness; produce it by a real act of your mind. Or do you find it otherwise?

I. I have virtually admitted this already. In addition to the consciousness which I find, I posit another which I do not find in myself: I thus complete and double my actual consciousness, and this is certainly an act. But I am tempted to take back either my admission or else the whole supposition. I am perfectly conscious of the act of my mind when I form a general conception, or when in cases of doubt I choose one of the many possible modes of action which lie before me; but of the act through which, according to your assertion, I must produce the presentation of an object external to me, I am not conscious at all.

Spirit. Do not be deceived. Of an act of your mind you can become conscious only in so far as you pass through a state of indetermination and indecision, of which you were likewise conscious, and to which this act puts an end. There is no such state of indecision in the case we have supposed; the mind has no need to deliberate what object it shall superadd to its particular sensations—it is done at once. We even find this distinction in philosophical phraseology. An act of the mind of which we are conscious as such is called "freedom." An act without consciousness of action is called "spontaneity." Remember that I by no means attribute to you an immediate consciousness of the act as such; it is rather that on subsequent reflection you discover that there must have been an act. The higher question, what it is that prevents any such state of indecision, or any consciousness of our act, will undoubtedly be afterwards solved.

This act of the mind is called "thought"—a word which I have hitherto employed with your concurrence; and it is said that thought takes place with spontaneity, in opposition to sensation which is mere receptivity. How is it then that, in your previous supposition, you add in thought to the sensation which you certainly have an object of which you know nothing?

I. I assume that my sensation must have a cause, and then proceed further.

Spirit. Will you not explain to me what is a cause?

I. I find a thing determined this way or that. I cannot rest satisfied with knowing that it *is* in this state. I assume that it has *become so,* and that not through itself, but by means of a foreign power. This foreign power, which made the thing what it is, *contains the cause;* and the manifestation of that power, which did actually make it so, *is the cause* of this particular determination of the thing. My sensation must have a cause: this means that the sensation is produced within me by a foreign power.

Spirit. In thought, you now add this foreign power to the sensation of which you are immediately conscious; thus arises in you the idea or presentation of an object? Well—let it be so.

Now observe: If sensation must have a cause, then I admit the correctness of your inference; and I see with what perfect right you assume the existence of external objects, notwithstanding that you neither know, nor *can* know, anything of them. But how then do you know, and how do you propose to prove, *that* sensation must have a cause? Or, in the general manner in which you have stated the proposition, why can you not rest satisfied to know that something *is?* Why must you assume that it has *become so,* or that it has become so by means of a foreign power? I note that you have always merely assumed this.

I. I confess it. But I cannot do otherwise than think so. It seems as if I knew it immediately.

Spirit. We will want to know what this answer, "I know it immediately," may signify, if we are brought back to it as the only possible one. But first we shall try all other possible methods of ascertaining the grounds of the assertion that everything must have a cause.

Do you know this by immediate perception?

I. How could I? Perception declares only that something in me *is,* according as I am determined this way or that, but never that it has *become so,* still less that it has become so by means of a foreign power lying beyond all perception.

Spirit. Or do you obtain this principle by generalization of your observation of external things, the cause of which you have always found to be something other than themselves—an observation which you now apply to yourself and to your own condition?

I. Do not treat me like a child and ascribe to me palpable absurdities. By the principle of causality I first arrive at a knowledge of things external to me; how then can I again, by observation of these things, arrive at this principle itself? Shall the earth rest on the great elephant and the great elephant rest again upon the earth?

Spirit. Or is this principle a deduction from some other general truth?

I. Which again could be founded neither on immediate perception, nor on the observation of external things, and concerning the origin of which you would still raise other questions! I could only possess this previous fundamental truth by immediate knowledge. Better to say this at once of the principle of causality and so put your conjectures aside.

Spirit. Let it be so; we then obtain, besides the first immediate knowledge of our own states through sensible perception, a second immediate knowledge concerning a general truth?

I. So it appears.

Spirit. The particular knowledge now in question—namely, that your affections or states must have a cause, is entirely independent of the knowledge of things?

I. Certainly, for the latter is itself obtained only by means of the former.

Spirit. And you have it absolutely in yourself?

I. Absolutely, for only by means of it do I first proceed outside of myself.

Spirit. Outside of yourself, therefore, and through yourself, and through your own immediate knowledge, you prescribe laws to being and its relations?

I. Rightly considered, I prescribe laws only to my own presentations of being and its relations; and it will be more correct to speak in this way.

Spirit. Be it so. Are you then conscious of these laws in any other way than by acting in accordance with them?

I. My consciousness begins with the perception of my own state; I connect this state directly with the presentation of an object, in accordance with the principle of causality. Both of these, the consciousness of my own state and the presentation of an object, are inseparably united; there is no intervening consciousness between them, and this one undivided consciousness is preceded by no other. No, it is impossible that I should be conscious of this law before acting in accordance with it, or in any other way than by so acting.

Spirit. You act upon this law, therefore, without being conscious of it; you act upon it immediately and absolutely.

But just now you declared yourself conscious of it, and expressed it as a general proposition. How have you arrived at this latter consciousness?

I. Doubtless in this way: I observe myself subsequently, and perceive that I have thus acted, and turn this common experience into a general law.

Spirit. You can, therefore, become conscious of this experience?

I. Unquestionably. I can guess the object of these questions. This is the above-mentioned second kind of immediate consciousness, that of my *activity;* as the first is sensation, or the consciousness of my *passivity.*

Spirit. Right. You *may* subsequently become conscious of your own acts, by free observation of yourself and by reflection; but it *is not necessary* that you should become so; at the moment of these internal acts, you are not immediately conscious of them.

I. Yet I must be originally conscious of them, for I am immediately conscious of my presentation of the object at the same moment that I am conscious of the sensation. I have found the solution: I am immediately conscious of my act, only not *as such;* but it moves before me as something presented. This consciousness is a consciousness of the object. Subsequently, by free reflection I may also become conscious of it as an act of my own mind.

My immediate consciousness is composed of two elements: the consciousness of my passivity, i.e., sensation; and that of my activity, in the production of an object according to the law of causality, the latter consciousness connecting itself immediately with the former. My consciousness of the object is merely an unrecognized *consciousness of my production of a presentation of an object.* I know of this production only because I myself am that which produces it. And thus all consciousness is immediate, is but a consciousness of myself, and therefore perfectly comprehensible. Do I follow you correctly?

Spirit. Perfectly so; but whence, then, the necessity and universality you have ascribed to your principles—in this case to the principle of causality?

I. From the immediate feeling that I cannot act otherwise, so surely as I have reason, and that no other reasonable being can act otherwise, so surely as it is a reasonable being. The principle that everything contingent—in the present case, my own sensation—must have a cause means this: "I have at all times added the supposition of a cause, and anyone who thinks is similarly constrained to add the supposition of a cause."

Spirit. You perceive then that all knowledge is merely a knowledge of yourself; that your consciousness never goes beyond yourself; and that what you assume to be a consciousness of the object is nothing but a consciousness of the fact that you have *posited* the object—posited it necessarily, in accordance with an inward law of your thought, at the same time as the sensation.

I. Proceed boldly with your inferences; I have not interrupted you, I have even helped you in the development of these conclusions. But now, seriously: I retract my whole previous position, that by means of the principle of causality I arrive at the knowledge of external things; and I did, indeed, inwardly retract it as soon as it led us into serious error.

In this way I could become conscious only of a mere *power* existing beyond myself, and of this only as a conception of my own mind; just as for the explanation of magnetic phenomena, I suppose a magnetic—or for the explanation of electrical phenomena, an electrical—power in Nature.

But the world does not appear to me such a mere thought, the thought of a mere power. It is something extended, something which is throughout accessible to experience—

accessible in itself, and not merely, as in the case of a power, through its manifestations. It does not *produce* attributes, as a power does; it *has* them. I am inwardly conscious of my apprehension of it, in a manner quite different from my consciousness of mere thought; it appears to me as perception, in spite of the proof that it cannot be such. It would be difficult for me to describe this kind of consciousness and to distinguish it from the other kinds of which we have spoken.

Spirit. You must nevertheless attempt such a description; otherwise I shall not understand you, and we shall never arrive at clearness.

I. I will attempt to open a way toward it. I beseech you, Spirit, if your organ of sight be like mine, to fix your eye on the red object before us, to surrender yourself unreservedly to the impression produced by it, and to forget meanwhile your previous conclusions. Now tell me candidly what takes place in your mind.

Spirit. I can completely put myself in your position; and it is no purpose of mine to disown any impression which has an actual existence. But tell me, what is the effect you anticipate?

I. Do you not perceive, and apprehend at a single glance, the surface? I say *the surface?* Does it not stand there present before you, entire and at once? Are you conscious, even in the most distant and obscure way, of this extension of a simple red point to a line, and of this line to a surface, of which you have spoken? It is an after-thought to divide this surface, and conceive of its points and lines. Would you not, and would not everyone who impartially observes himself, maintain and insist, notwithstanding your former conclusions, that he really *saw* a surface of such or such a color?

Spirit. I admit all this; and, on examining myself, I find that it is exactly as you have described.

But, in the first place, have you forgotten that it is not our object to relate to each other what presents itself in consciousness, as in a journal of the human mind, but to consider its various phenomena in their connection, and to explain them by, and deduce them from, each other; and that consequently none of your observations—which certainly cannot be denied and which must instead be explained—can overturn any one of my just conclusions?

I. I shall never lose sight of this.

Spirit. Then, when you consider the remarkable resemblance which this consciousness of external things bears to real perception, do not overlook the great difference which nevertheless exists between them.

I. I was about to mention this difference. Each type of consciousness appears as immediate, not as acquired or produced. But sensation is consciousness of my own state. Not so the consciousness of the object itself, which has absolutely no reference to me. I know that it *is,* and this is all; it does not apply to me. If, in the first case, I seem like a piece of soft clay, pressed and molded now in this way, now in that, then, in the second, I appear like a mirror before which objects pass without producing the slightest change in the mirror itself.

This distinction, however, is in my favor. Just so much the more do I seem to have a distinct consciousness of a being beyond myself, entirely independent of the sense of my own state of being; I speak of a being beyond myself, for this latter consciousness is altogether different from the consciousness of my own internal states.

Spirit. You observe well, but do not rush too hastily to a conclusion.

If that whereon we have already agreed remains true and you can be immediately conscious of yourself alone; if the consciousness now in question is not a consciousness of your own passivity and still less a consciousness of your own activity, may it not then be an unrecognized consciousness of your own being?—of your being in so far as you are a *knowing* being, or an Intelligence?

I. I do not understand you; but help me once more, for I wish to understand.

Spirit. I must then demand your whole attention, for I am here compelled to go deeper and expatiate more widely than ever.

What are you?

I. To answer your question in the most general way: I am I, myself.

Spirit. I am well satisfied with this answer. What do you mean when you say "I"—what lies in this conception and how do you attain it?

I. On this point I can make myself understood only by contrast. External existence—*the thing*—is something outside of me, the knower. I am *myself* the knower, and am one with that which knows. As to my consciousness of external existence, there arises the question: since the thing cannot know itself, how can a knowledge of it arise? How can a consciousness of the thing arise *in me*, since I myself am not the thing, nor any of its modes or forms, and since all these modes and forms lie within the circle of its own being, and by no means in mine? How does the thing reach me? What is the tie between me, the subject, and the thing which is the object of my knowledge? But as to my consciousness of *myself*, there can be no such questions. In this case, I have my knowledge within myself, for I am intelligence. What I am, I know because I am it; and I am that which I immediately know myself to be precisely because I do know it. There is here no need of any tie between subject and object; my own nature is this tie. I am subject and object: and this *subject-objectivity*, this return of knowledge upon itself, is what I mean by the term "I," when I deliberately attach a definite meaning to it.

Spirit. Thus it is in the identity of subject and object that your nature as an intelligence consists?

I. Yes.

Spirit. Can you then comprehend the possibility of your becoming conscious of this identity, which is neither subject nor object, but which lies at the foundation of both, and out of which both arise?

I. By no means. It is the condition of all my consciousness that the conscious being, and what he is conscious of, appear distinct and separate. I cannot even conceive of any other consciousness. In the very act of recognizing myself, I recognize myself as subject and object, both however being immediately bound up with each other.

Spirit. Can you become conscious of the moment in which this inconceivable one separated itself into these two?

I. How can I, since my consciousness first becomes possible in and through their separation, since it is my consciousness itself that thus separates them? Beyond consciousness itself there is no consciousness.

Spirit. It is this separation, then, that you necessarily recognize in becoming conscious of yourself? In this your original being consists?

I. That is true.

Spirit. And on what then is this separation founded?

I. I am intelligence, and have consciousness of myself. This separation is the condition and result of consciousness. It has its foundation, therefore, in myself, like consciousness.

Spirit. You are intelligence, you say, at least this is all that is now in question, and as such you become an object to yourself. Your knowledge therefore, *as objective,* presents itself before you, i.e., before your knowledge, *as subjective,* and floats before it; but without you yourself being conscious of such a presentation?

I. That is true.

Spirit. Can you not then adduce some more exact characteristics of the subjective and objective elements as they appear in consciousness?

I. The subjective appears to contain within itself the foundation of consciousness as regards its form, but not as regards its substance. That there is a consciousness, an inward perception and conception—of this the cause or foundation lies in itself. But that precisely this or that is conceived—the consciousness of *this* is dependent on the objective, with which it is conjoined, and with which it, as it were, passes away. The objective, on the contrary, contains the foundation of its being within itself; it is in and for itself—it is as it is because it is so. The subjective appears as the still and passive mirror of the objective; the latter floats before it. That the subjective should reflect images—of this the cause or foundation lies in itself. That precisely this image and none other should be reflected, this depends upon the objective.

Spirit. The *subjective,* then, according to its essential nature, is constituted in just the way in which you have described your own consciousness of external existence?

I. That is true, and this agreement is remarkable. I begin to find it half credible that out of the internal laws of my own consciousness may proceed even the presentation of an external existence which is independent of myself; and that this presentation may at bottom be nothing more than the presentation of these laws themselves.

Spirit. And why only half credible?

I. Because I do not yet see why precisely such a presentation—a presentation of a mass extended through space—should arise.

Spirit. You have already seen that it is only your own sensation which you extend through space; and you have suspected that it is by this extension in space alone that your sensation becomes transformed into something sensible. We have therefore to do at present only with space itself, and to explain its origin in consciousness.

I. That is true.

Spirit. Let us then make the attempt. I know that you cannot become conscious of your intelligent activity as such, in so far as it remains in its original and unchangeable unity—in the condition which begins with its very being, and can never be destroyed without at the same time destroying that being. Hence I do not ascribe such a consciousness to you. But you can become conscious of it in so far as it passes from one state of transition to another within the limits of this unchangeable unity. When you represent it to yourself in the performance of this function, how does this internal spiritual activity appear to you?

I. My spiritual faculty appears as if in a state of internal motion—swiftly passing from one point to another; in short, it appears to me as an extended line. A definite thought makes a point in this line.

Spirit. And why as an extended line?

I. Can I give a reason for that without overstepping the limits of my own existence and stepping outside the circle beyond which I cannot go? The thing is merely so.

Spirit. It is in this way, then, that a particular act of your consciousness appears to you. But what shape, then, is assumed by that knowledge—inherited, but not produced, by you—of which all specific thought is but the revival and further definition? How does this present itself to you?

I. Evidently as something in which one may draw lines and make points in all directions, namely, *as space.*

Spirit. And now it will be entirely clear to you how that which really proceeds from yourself may nevertheless appear to you as an existence external to yourself—and must necessarily appear in this way.

You have now reached the true source of the presentation of things. This presentation is not perception, for you perceive only yourself; nor is it thought, for things do not appear to you as mere results of thought. It is an actual and, indeed, absolute and immediate consciousness of an existence external to yourself, just as perception is an immediate consciousness of your own condition. Do not permit yourself to be perplexed by sophists and half-philosophers; things do not appear to you through any representation; of the thing which is there, and can be there, you are immediately conscious; and there is no other thing than that of which you are conscious. You yourself are the thing; you yourself, by virtue of your finitude—the innermost law of your being—are thus presented before yourself, and projected out of yourself; and all that you perceive beyond yourself is still yourself alone. This consciousness has been well named "intuition." In all consciousness I am intuitively aware of myself; for I am myself: for the subjective, conscious being, consciousness is intuitive self-contemplation. And the objective, that which is contemplated and of which I am conscious, is also myself—the same self which contemplates, but which now floats as an objective presentation before the subjective. In this respect, consciousness is an active retrospect of my own intuitions; an observation of myself from my own position; a projection of myself out of myself by means of the only mode of action which is properly mine—intuitive consciousness. I am a living faculty of vision. My seeing is what I see; my consciousness is what I am conscious of.[1]

Hence this thing is also thoroughly transparent to your mind's eye, because it is itself you. You divide, limit, and determine the possible forms of things, and the relations of these forms, previous to all perception. No wonder; for in so doing you divide, limit, and determine your own knowledge, which undoubtedly is sufficiently known to you. In this way a knowledge of things becomes possible; it is

[1] ["*Ich sehe—Bewusstsein—sehe mein Sehen—bewusstes.*"]

not in the things, and cannot proceed out of them. It proceeds from you, and is indeed your own nature.

There is no outward sense, for there is no outward perception. There is, however, an outward intuition—but not of things. This outward intuition—this knowledge apparently external to the subjective being, and hovering before it—is itself the thing, and there is no other. By means of this outward intuition are perception and sense regarded as external. It remains eternally true, for it is proved: I never [2] see or feel a surface; but I intuitively apprehend my seeing, or feeling, as seeing or feeling of a surface. Space—illuminated, transparent, palpable, penetrable space—the purest image of my knowledge, is not seen, but is intuited. And in it my seeing itself is intuited. The light is not outside of me, it is within me, and I myself am the light. You have already answered my question, "How do you know of your sensations, of your seeing, feeling, etc.?" by saying that you have an immediate knowledge or consciousness of them. Now, perhaps, you will be able to define more exactly this immediate consciousness of sensation.

I. It must be a two-fold consciousness. Sensation is itself an immediate consciousness; for I am sensible of my own sensation. But from this there arises no knowledge of outward existence, but only *the feeling of my own state.* I am however, originally, not merely a sensitive, but also an intuitive being; not merely a practical being, but also an intelligence. I intuitively contemplate my sensation itself, and thus there arises from myself and my own nature the knowledge *of an existence.* Sensation becomes transformed into its own object; my affections, as red, smooth, and the like, into a *something* red, smooth etc., external to myself; and this something, and my relative sensation, I intuitively contemplate in space, because the intuition itself is space. Thus it becomes clear why I believe that I see or feel sur-

2 [Reading *"immer"* as *"niemals".*]

faces which, in fact, I neither see nor feel. I intuitively regard my own sensation of sight or touch as the sight or touch of a surface.

Spirit. You have well understood me or, rather, yourself.

I. But now it is not by means of any inference from the principle of causality, either recognized or unrecognized, that things are originated for me; they float immediately before me, and are presented to my consciousness without any process of reasoning. I cannot say, as I have formerly said, that perception becomes transformed into something perceivable, for the perceivable, as such, has precedence in consciousness. Consciousness does not begin with an affection of myself, as red, smooth, or the like; it begins with a red, smooth object external to myself.

Spirit. If, however, you were obliged to explain what this red, smooth, and the like, is, could you possibly make any other reply than that it is that which affects you in a certain manner?

I. Certainly not—if you were to ask me, and I were to enter upon the question and attempt an explanation. But originally no one asks me the question, nor do I ask it of myself. I forget myself entirely and lose myself in my intuition of the object; I become conscious, not of my own state, but only of an existence beyond myself. Red, green, and the like, are properties of the thing; it is red or green, and this is all. There can be no further explanation, any more than there can be a further explanation of these affections in me—on this we have already agreed. This is most obvious in the sensation of sight: color appears as something external to myself. The common understanding of man, if left to itself, and without further reflection, could hardly be persuaded to describe red, green, etc., as that which excited a specific internal affection.

Spirit. But, doubtless, it might so describe sweet or sour.

It is not our business at present to inquire whether the impression made by means of sight is a pure sensation, or whether it may not rather be a middle term between sensation and intuition, and the bond by which they are united in our minds. But I admit your assertion, and it is extremely welcome to me. You can, indeed, lose yourself in the intuition; and unless you direct particular attention to yourself, or take an interest in some external action, you do thus lose yourself naturally and necessarily. This is the remark to which the defenders of a groundless consciousness of external things appeal when it is shown that the principle of causality, by which the existence of such things might be inferred, exists only in ourselves; they deny that any such inference is made, and, in so far as they refer to actual consciousness in particular cases, this cannot be disputed. These same defenders, when the nature of intuition is explained to them in terms of the laws of intelligence itself, draw this inference anew themselves and never weary of repeating that there must be something external to us which compels us to this belief.

I. Do not trouble yourself about them at present, but instruct me. I have no preconceived opinion, but seek for truth only.

Spirit. Nevertheless, intuition necessarily proceeds from the perception of your own state, although, as you have already seen, you are not always clearly conscious of this perception. Even in that consciousness in which you lose yourself in the object, there is always something which is possible only by means of an unrecognized reference to yourself and close observation of your own state.

I. Consequently, at all times and places the consciousness of external existence must be accompanied by an unobserved consciousness of myself?

Spirit. Just so.

I. The former being determined through the latter—determined as it actually is?

Spirit. That is my meaning.

I. Show me this and I shall be satisfied.

Spirit. Do you place things generally only in space, or do you place each thing in a determinate position of space?

I. The latter—each thing has its determinate size.

Spirit. And do different things occupy the same part of space?

I. By no means; they exclude each other. They are beside, over or under, behind or before, each other—nearer to me or farther from me.

Spirit. And how do you come to this measurement and arrangement of them in space? Is it by sensation?

I. How could that be, since space itself is no sensation?

Spirit. Or intuition?

I. This cannot be. Intuition is immediate and infallible. What is contained in it does not appear as produced, and cannot deceive. But I must train myself to estimate, measure, and deliberate upon the size of an object, its distance from me, its position with respect to other objects. It is a truth known to every beginner that we originally see all objects in the same line; that we learn to estimate their greater or lesser distances; that the child attempts to grasp distant objects as if they lay immediately before his eyes; and that one born blind who should suddenly receive sight would do the same. This conception of distances is therefore a judgment—no intuition, but an ordering of my different intuitions by means of the understanding. I may err in my estimate of the size, distance, etc. of an object; and the so-called optical deceptions are not deceptions of sight, but erroneous judgments formed concerning the size of the object, concerning the size of its different parts in relation to each other, and consequently concerning its true figure and its distance from me and from other objects. But it does really exist in space, as I contemplate it, and the colors which I see in it are likewise really seen by me—and here there is no deception.

Spirit. And what then is the principle of this judgment? To take the most distinct and easy case—your judgment of the proximity or distance of objects: how do you estimate this distance?

I. Doubtless by the greater strength or weakness of impressions otherwise equal. I see before me two objects of the same red color. The one whose color I see more vividly, I regard as the nearer; that whose color seems to me fainter, as the more distant and as so much the more distant as the color seems fainter.

Spirit. Thus you estimate the distance according to the degree of strength or weakness in the sensation; and this strength or weakness itself—do you also estimate it?

I. Obviously only in so far as I take note of my own affections, and even of very slight differences in these. You have me! All consciousness of external objects is determined by the clearness and exactitude of my consciousness of my own states, and in this consciousness there is always a conclusion drawn from the effect in myself to a cause external to me.

Spirit. You give up quickly. I must now continue, in your place, the controversy against myself. My argument can apply only to those cases in which an actual and deliberate estimate of the size, distance, and position of objects takes place, and in which you are conscious of making such an estimate. You will, however, admit that this is by no means the common case, and that for the most part you become conscious of the size, distance, etc. of an object at the very same undivided moment in which you become conscious of the object itself.

I. When once we learn to estimate the distances of objects by the strength of the impression, the rapidity of this judgment is merely the consequence of its frequent exercise. I have learned, by a lifelong experience, to observe the strength of the impression rapidly and thereby to estimate the distance. My present conception is founded upon a combination, formerly made, of sensation, intuition, and previous judgments, although at the moment I am conscious only of the present conception. I no longer apprehend red, green, or the like, as being merely external to me, but a red or a green *at this, that, or the other distance;* but this last addition is merely a renewal of a judgment formerly arrived at by deliberate reflection.

Spirit. Has it now become clear whether you discover the existence of external things by intuition, or by reasoning, or both—and in how far by each of these?

I. Perfectly; and I believe that I have now attained the fullest insight into the origin of the presentation of external things:

1. I am absolutely conscious of myself, because I am this I—myself; and that partly as a practical being, partly as an intelligence. The first consciousness is sensation, the second intuition, of unlimited space.
2. I cannot comprehend the unlimited, for I am finite. I therefore set apart, in thought, a certain portion of universal space and place this portion in a certain relation to the whole.
3. The measure of this limited portion of space is the extent of my own sensibility, according to a principle which may be expressed in this way: whatever affects me in such or such a manner is to be placed in space in such and such relations to the other things which affect me.

The properties or attributes of the object proceed from the perception of my own internal state; the space which it fills, from intuitive contemplation. By a process of thought, both are conjoined—the former being added to the latter. What we have said before is assuredly so: that which is merely a state or affection of myself, by being transferred or projected into space, becomes an attribute of the object; but it is so projected into space, not by intuition, but by thought, by measuring and ordering thought. This act is not to be regarded as an intellectual discovery or creation; it is only as a more exact determination, by means of thought, of something which is already given in sensation and intuition, independent of all thought.

Spirit. Whatever affects me in such or such a manner is to be placed in such or such relations: this is the way you reason in bounding and arranging objects in space. But does the assertion that a thing affects you in a certain manner include the assumption that it affects you generally?

I. Undoubtedly.

Spirit. And is any presentation of an external object possible which is not in this manner limited and defined in space?

I. No; for no object exists in space generally, but each one in a determinate portion of space.

Spirit. So that in fact, whether you are conscious of it or not, every external object is assumed by you as affecting yourself, as certainly as it is assumed as filling a determinate portion of space?

I. That follows, certainly.

Spirit. And what kind of presentation is that of an object affecting yourself?

I. Evidently a thought; and, indeed, a thought founded on the principle of causality already mentioned. I see now, still more clearly, that the consciousness of the object is engrafted on my self-consciousness in two ways—partly by intuition, and partly by thought founded on the principle of causality. The object, however strange this may seem, is at once the immediate object of my consciousness and also the result of deliberate thought.

Spirit. In different respects, however. You must be capable of being conscious of this thought of the object?

I. Doubtless; although usually I am not so.

Spirit. Therefore, to your passive state, your affection,

you add in thought an activity external to yourself—such as you described earlier in the case of thought, in accordance with the principle of causality?

I. Yes.

Spirit. And with the same meaning and the same validity as you described it before. You think so once for all, and must think so; you cannot alter it, and can know nothing more than that you do think so?

I. Nothing more. We have already investigated all this thoroughly.

Spirit. You assume an object. In so far as it is so assumed, is it a product of your thought alone?

I. Certainly; this follows from what we have said.

Spirit. And what now is this object which is thus assumed according to the principle of causality?

I. A power external to myself.

Spirit. Which is an object neither of sensation nor of intuition?

I. It is an object of neither; I remain perfectly conscious that I do not perceive it immediately, but only by means of its manifestations; although I ascribe to it an existence independent of myself. I am affected; there must, therefore, be something that affects me: such is my thought.

Spirit. The object which is intuited and that which you assume by reasoning are thus very different things. That which is actually and immediately present before you, spread out in space, is the object of intuition; the internal force within it, which is not present before you, but whose existence you are led to assert only by a process of inference, is the object of the reason.

I. You say the internal force within it; I now think you are right. I place this force also in space and add it to the mass which I regard as occupying space.

Spirit. And what then, according to your view, is the nature of the relation between this force and the mass?

I. The mass, with its properties, is itself the result and manifestation of the inward force. This force has two modes of operation: one whereby it maintains itself and assumes the particular form in which it appears; another upon me, by which it affects me in a particular manner.

Spirit. Formerly you were looking for another bearer of sensible attributes or qualities—something other than the space which contains them, this space which is permanent amid the vicissitudes of perpetual change?

I. Yes, and this permanent thing is found. It is force itself. This remains forever the same amid all change, and it is this which assumes and supports all sensible attributes or qualities.

Spirit. Let us look back on all that we have found. You feel yourself in a certain state, affected in a certain manner, which you call red, smooth, sweet, and so on. Of this you know only that you feel, and feel in this particular manner. Or do you know more than this? Is there in mere feeling anything more than mere feeling?

I. No.

Spirit. Further, it is the determination of your own nature as an intelligence that is spread out before you as space. Or do you know something more than this concerning space?

I. By no means.

Spirit. Between that felt condition, and this space which is spread out before you, there is not the smallest connection except that they are both present in your consciousness. Or do you perceive still another connection between them?

I. I see none.

Spirit. But you are a thinking, as well as a sensitive and intuitive, being; and yet you know nothing more of this matter than that you are this. You do not merely feel your sensible state; you can also conceive of it in thought; but it provides no complete thought; you are compelled to add something to it, an external foundation, a foreign power. Or do you know more of it than just the fact that you do so think and are compelled so to think?

I. I can know nothing more respecting it. I cannot proceed beyond my thought; for, simply because I think it, it becomes my thought and falls under the inevitable laws of my being.

Spirit. Through this thought of yours, there first arises a connection between your own state which you feel and the space which you intuitively contemplate; you suppose the one the foundation of the other. Is this not so?

I. It is so. You have clearly proved that I produce this connection in my consciousness by my own thought only, and that such a connection is neither directly felt, nor intuitively perceived. But of any connection *beyond the limits of my consciousness* I cannot speak; I cannot even describe such a connection in any way; for even in speaking of it I must know of it, and, since this consciousness can be only a thought, I thus think of it; and this is precisely the same connection which occurs in my ordinary natural consciousness, and no other. I cannot proceed a hair's breadth beyond this consciousness, any more than I can spring out of myself. All attempts to conceive of an absolute connection between things *in themselves* and the I *in itself* are but attempts to ignore our own thought, a strange forgetfulness of the undeniable fact that we can have no thought without having thought it. That there is a thing *in itself* is itself a thought; namely, this, that there is a great thought which yet no man has ever thought out.

Spirit. From you, then, I need fear no objection to the principle now established: that *our consciousness of external things is absolutely nothing more than the product of our own presentative faculty,* and that, with respect to such things, we know only what is produced through our consciousness itself, through a determinate consciousness subject to definite laws.

I. I cannot refute this. It is so.

Spirit. You cannot object, then, to the bolder statement of the same proposition: that, in what we call knowledge and observation of outward things, we at all times recognize and observe ourselves only; and that in all our consciousness we know of nothing whatever but of ourselves and of our own determinate states.

I say you will not be able to make any objection to this proposition; for if the external world *generally* arises for us only through our own consciousness, what is *particular* and *multiform* in this external world must arise in this same way; and if the connection between what is external to us and ourselves is merely a connection in our own thought, then the connection of the multifarious objects of the external world *among themselves* is undoubtedly this and no other. I have pointed out to you the origin of this system of external objects, and their relation to you; now, with like clarity, I could also show you the law according to which there arises an infinite multiplicity of such objects, mutually connected, reciprocally determining each other with rigid necessity, and thus forming a complete world-system, as you yourself have well described it; and I spare myself this task only because I find that you have already admitted the conclusion for the sake of which alone I should have undertaken it.

I. I see it all, and must assent to it.

Spirit. And with this insight, mortal, be free and forever released from the fear which has degraded and tormented you! You will no longer tremble at a necessity which exists only in your own thought; no longer fear to be crushed by things which are the product of your own mind; no longer place yourself, the thinking being, in the same class with the thoughts which proceed from you. As long as you could believe that a system of things, such as you have described, really existed outside of, and independently of, yourself, and that you yourself might be merely a link in this chain, such a fear was well grounded. Now, when you have seen that all this exists only in and through yourself, you will doubtless no longer fear that which you now recognize as your own creation.

It was from this fear that I wished to set you free. You are delivered from it, and I now leave you to yourself.

I. Stay, deceitful Spirit! Is this all the wisdom toward which you have directed my hopes, and do you boast that you have set me free? You have set me free, it is true; you have absolved me from all dependence, for you have transformed me, and everything around me on which I could possibly be dependent, into nothing. You have abolished necessity by annihilating all existence.

Spirit. Is the danger so great?

I. And you can jest! According to your system—

Spirit. My system? Whatever we have agreed upon, we have produced in common; we have labored together, and you have understood everything as well as I myself. But it would still be difficult for you at present even to guess at my true and perfect mode of thought.

I. Call your thoughts by what name you will; by all that you have hitherto said, there is nothing, absolutely nothing but presentations—modes of consciousness, and of consciousness only. But a presentation is to me only the picture, the shadow, of a reality; in itself it cannot satisfy me and has not the smallest worth. I might be content that this material world beyond me should vanish into a mere picture, or be dissolved into a shadow; I am not dependent on it. But according to your previous reasoning, I myself disappear no less than it; I myself am transformed into a mere presentation, without meaning and without purpose. Or tell me, is it otherwise?

Spirit. I say nothing in my own name. Examine—help yourself!

I. I appear to myself as a body existing in space, with organs of sense and of action, as a physical force governed by a will. Of all this you will say—as you previously said of objects external to me, the thinking being—that it is a product of sensation, intuition, and thought combined.

Spirit. Undoubtedly. I will even show you, step by step, if you desire it, the laws according to which you appear to yourself in consciousness as an organic body, with such and such senses, as a physical force, etc., and you will be compelled to admit the truth of what I show you.

I. I foresee that result. As I have been compelled to admit that what I call sweet, red, hard, and so on, is nothing more than my own affection; and that only by intuition and thought it is transposed out of myself into space and regarded as the property of something existing independently of me; so also shall I be compelled to admit that this body, with all its organs, is nothing but a sensible manifestation, in a determinate portion of space, of myself the inward thinking being; that I, the spiritual entity, the pure intelligence, and I, the bodily frame in the physical world, are one and the same, merely viewed from two different sides and conceived of by two different faculties—the first, by pure thought; the second, by external intuition.

Spirit. This would certainly be the result of any inquiry that might be instituted.

I. And this thinking spiritual entity, this intelligence which by intuition is transformed into a material body—what can even it be, according to these principles, but a product of my own thought, something merely conceived of by me because I am compelled to imagine its existence by virtue of a law to me wholly incomprehensible, proceeding from nothing and tending to nothing?

Spirit. It is possible.

I. You become hesitating and monosyllabic. It is not only possible; it is necessary according to these principles.

This perceiving, thinking, willing, intelligent entity, or

whatever else you may name that which possesses the faculties of perception, thought, and so forth—that in which these faculties inhere, or in whatever other way you may express this thought: how do I attain a knowledge of it? Am I immediately conscious of it? How can I be? It is only of actual and specific *acts* of perception, thought, will etc., as of particular occurrences, that I am immediately conscious; not of the capacities through which they are performed, and still less of a being in whom these capacities inhere. I perceive, directly and intuitively, this specific thought which occupies me during the present moment, and other specific thoughts in other moments; and here this inward intellectual intuition, this immediate consciousness, ends. This inward intuitive thought now becomes itself an object of thought; but, according to the laws under which alone I can think, it seems to me imperfect and incomplete, just as formerly the thought of my sensible states was but an imperfect thought. A while ago I made, in thought, an unconscious addition of an active element to mere passivity. Now, in like manner, I add to my determinate state (my actual thought or will) a determinable element *(an infinite, possible thought or will)*. I *must* do this, and for the same reason in both cases, but without being conscious of this mental addition as such. This manifold possible thought I further comprehend as one definite whole—once more because I must do so, since I am unable to comprehend anything indefinite. In this way I obtain the idea of a *finite capacity of thought* and—since this idea carries with it the notion of a something independent of the thought itself—of a being or entity which possesses this capacity.

But on higher principles it becomes still more conceivable how this thinking being is produced by its own thought. Thought in itself is genetic, assuming the previous creation of an object immediately revealed, and occupying itself with the description of this object. Intuition gives the naked fact, and nothing more. Thought explains this fact and unites it to another, not found in intuition, but produced purely by thought itself, from which it, the fact, proceeds. So, too, in this case, I am conscious of a determinate thought; thus far, and no farther, does intuitive consciousness carry me. I *think* this determinate thought, that is, I bring it forth from an indeterminate, but determinable, possibility of thought. In this way I proceed with anything determinate which is presented in immediate consciousness, and thus arise for me all those series of capacities, and of beings possessing these capacities, whose existence I assume.

Spirit. Even with respect to yourself, therefore, you are conscious only that you feel, perceive, or think in this or that determinate manner?

I. That I feel, I perceive, I think?—that I, as the efficient principle, produce the sensation, the intuition, the thought? By no means! Your principles have not even left me with this much.

Spirit. Possibly.

I. Necessarily; for see: all that I know is my consciousness itself. All consciousness is either an immediate or a mediate consciousness. The first is self-consciousness; the second, consciousness of that which is not myself. What I call *I* is, therefore, absolutely nothing more than a certain modification of consciousness which is called *I,* just because it is immediate, returning into itself, and not directed outward. Since all other consciousness is possible only under the condition of this immediate consciousness, it is obvious that this consciousness which is called *I* must accompany all my other conceptions, be necessarily contained in them, although not always clearly perceived by me, and that in each moment of my consciousness I must refer everything to this I, and not to the particular thing external to me thought of at the moment. In this way the I would at every moment vanish and reappear; and for every new conception

a new I would arise, and this I would never signify anything more than—what is *not the thing*.

This scattered self-consciousness is now combined by
thought—by mere thought, I say—and presented in the unity
of a supposed capacity of thought. According to this supposition, all conceptions which are accompanied by the immediate consciousness already spoken of must proceed from
one and the same capacity, which inheres in one and the
same entity; and thus there arises for me the notion of the
identity and personality of my I, and of an efficient and
real power in this person—necessarily a mere fiction, since
this capacity and this entity are only feigned.

Spirit. You reason correctly.

I. And you have pleasure in this! I may then indeed say
"it is thought,"—and yet I can scarcely say even this. Strictly
speaking, I ought to say *"the thought appears* that I feel,
perceive, think," and not "*I* feel, perceive, think." The first
only is fact; the second is an imaginary addition to the fact.

Spirit. It is well expressed.

I. There is nothing enduring, either external to me or in
me, but only ceaseless change. I know of no being, not even
of my own. There is no being. I myself absolutely know not,
and am not. Pictures are: they are the only things which
exist, and they know of themselves after the fashion of pictures; pictures which float past without there being anything
past which they float; which, by means of like pictures, are
connected with each other; pictures without anything which
is pictured in them, without significance and without aim.
I myself am one of these pictures; nay, I am not even this,
but merely a confused picture of the pictures. All reality
is transformed into a strange dream, without a life which
is dreamed of, and without a mind which dreams it; into a
dream which is woven together in a dream of itself. Intuition is dream; thought—the source of all the being and all
the reality I picture, the source of *my own* being, my own
powers, and my own purposes—is the dream of that dream.

Spirit. You have well understood it all. Employ the sharpest expressions to make this result hateful, since you must submit to it. And this you must do. You have clearly seen that it cannot be otherwise. Or will you now retract your admissions and justify your retraction on principle?

I. By no means. I have seen, and now see clearly, that it is so; yet I cannot believe it.

Spirit. You see it clearly, and yet can *not* believe it? That is a different matter.

I. You are a profligate spirit: your knowledge itself is profligacy, and springs from profligacy; and I cannot thank you for having led me on this path!

Spirit. Short-sighted mortal! When men venture to look into being and see as far as themselves, and a little farther—you call it profligacy. I have allowed you to deduce the results of our inquiry in your own way, to analyze them, and to clothe them in hateful expressions. Did you then think that these results were less known to me than to yourself, that I did not understand, as well as you do, how by these principles all reality was thoroughly annihilated and transformed into a dream? Did you then take me for a blind admirer and advocate of this system, as a complete system of the human mind?

You wanted to *know,* and you took a wrong road. You looked for knowledge where no knowledge can reach, and you even persuaded yourself that you had obtained an insight into something which is opposed to the very nature of all insight. I found you in this condition. I wished to free you from your false knowledge; but by no means to bring you the true.

You wanted to know of your knowledge. Are you surprised that in this way you discovered nothing more than that of which you wanted to know, your knowledge itself; and would you have had it otherwise? What has its origin in and through knowledge is merely knowledge. But all knowledge is only pictures, representations; and there is always something wanting in it—that which corresponds to the representation. This want cannot be supplied by knowledge; a system of knowledge is necessarily a system of mere pictures, wholly without reality, significance, or aim. Did you expect anything else? Would you change the very nature of your mind, and desire your knowledge to be something more than knowledge?

The reality, in which you formerly believed—a material world existing independently of you, of which you feared to become the slave—has vanished; for this whole material world arises only through knowledge, and is itself our knowledge. But knowledge is not reality—just because it is knowledge. You have seen through the illusion; and without belying your better insight, you can never again give yourself up to it. This is the sole merit which I claim for the system which we have together discovered; it destroys and annihilates error. It cannot give us truth, for in itself it is absolutely empty. You now seek, and with good right as I well know, something real lying beyond mere appearance, another reality than that which has thus been annihilated. But in vain would you labor to create this reality by means of your knowledge, or out of your knowledge; or to embrace it by your understanding. If you have no other means by which to apprehend it, you will never find it.

But you have such a means. Arouse and animate it, and you will attain to perfect tranquility. I leave you alone with yourself.

BOOK THREE

FAITH

Terrible Spirit, your discourse has smitten me to the ground. But you have referred me to myself. And what would I be if anything external to me could irrecoverably cast me down? I will—yes, I will surely follow your counsel.

What do you seek, then, my complaining heart? What is it that causes you to rebel against a system to which my understanding cannot raise the slightest objection?

This it is: I demand something beyond a mere presentation or conception; something that is, has been, and will be, even if the presentation were not; and which the presentation only records, without producing it, or in the smallest degree changing it. A mere presentation I now see to be a deceptive show; my presentations must have a meaning beneath them, and if all my knowledge revealed to me nothing but knowledge, I would be defrauded of my whole life. That there is nothing whatever but my presentations is, to the natural sense of mankind, a silly and ridiculous conceit which no man can seriously entertain and which requires no refutation. To the well-informed judge, who knows the deeper grounds for this opinion, grounds which cannot be removed by mere reasoning, this thought is one of despair and annihilation.

And what, then, is this something lying beyond all presentation, toward which I stretch forward with such ardent longing? What is the power with which it draws me toward it? What is the central point in my soul with which it is so intimately bound up and with which alone it can be destroyed?

"Your vocation is not merely to *know*, but to *act* according to your knowledge"; this is loudly proclaimed in the innermost depths of my soul, as soon as I recollect myself for a moment and turn my observation inward upon my self. "You are here, not for idle contemplation of yourself, or for brooding over devout sensations—no, you are here for action; your action, and your action alone, determines your worth."

This voice leads me out from presentation, from mere knowing, to something that is beyond it and opposed to it—to something that is greater and higher than all knowledge, and that contains within itself the end and object of all knowledge. When I act, I doubtless know that I act, and how I act; nevertheless this knowledge is not the act itself, but only the observation of it. This voice thus announces to me precisely that which I sought; a something lying beyond mere knowledge and, in its nature, wholly independent of knowledge.

Thus it is, I know it immediately. But I have entered within the domain of speculation and the doubt which has been awakened within me will secretly endure and continue to disturb me. Since I have placed myself in this position, I can obtain no complete satisfaction until everything which I accept is justified before the tribunal of speculation. I have thus to ask myself: how is it so? Whence arises that voice in my soul which directs me to something beyond mere presentation and knowledge?

There is within me an impulse to absolute, independent self-activity. Nothing is more insupportable to me than to exist merely by another, for another, and through another; I must be something for myself and by myself alone. This impulse I feel along with the perception of my own existence, it is inseparably united to my consciousness of myself.

I explain this feeling to myself by reflection; and, as it were, endow this blind impulse with the gift of insight. According to this impulse I must act as an absolutely independent being—thus I understand and translate the impulse. I must be independent. Who am I? Subject and object in one—the conscious being and that of which I am conscious, gifted with intuitive knowledge and myself revealed in that intuition, the thinking mind and myself the object of the thought—inseparable and ever present to each other. As both, I must be what I am, absolutely by myself alone; by myself originate conceptions, by myself produce a condition of things lying beyond these conceptions. But how is the latter possible? With nothing I cannot connect any being whatsoever; from nothing there can never arise something; my objective thought is necessarily mediative only. But any being that is connected with another being becomes thereby dependent; it is no longer a primary, original, and genetic, but only a secondary and derived, being. I am constrained to connect myself with something; I cannot connect myself with another being without losing that independence which is the condition of my own existence.

My conception and origination of a *purpose,* however, is, by its very nature, absolutely free—and producing something out of nothing. With such a conception I must connect my activity if the action is to be regarded as free and as proceeding absolutely from myself alone.

In the following manner, therefore, I conceive of my independence as I. I ascribe to myself the power of originating a conception simply because I originate it, of originating *this* conception simply because I originate *this* one—by the absolute sovereignty of myself as an intelligence. I further ascribe to myself the power of manifesting this conception beyond itself by means of an action; I ascribe to myself a real, active power, capable of producing something beyond itself, a power which is entirely different from the mere power of conception. These conceptions, which are called conceptions of design, or purposes, are not, like the conceptions of mere knowledge, copies of something already existing, but rather types of something yet to be; the real power lies beyond them, and is *in itself* independent of them; it receives from them only its immediate determinations, which are apprehended by knowledge. Such an independent power it is that, in consequence of this impulse, I ascribe to myself.

Here then, it appears, is the point at which consciousness connects itself with reality; the real efficiency of my conception, and the real power of action which, in consequence of it, I am compelled to ascribe to myself, is this point. Let it be as it may with the reality of a sensible world beyond me; I possess reality and comprehend it—it lies within my own being and is native to myself.

I conceive this, my real power of action, in thought, but I do not create it by thought. The immediate feeling of my impulse to independent activity lies at the foundation of this thought; the thought does no more than portray this feeling and accept it in its own form, the form of thought. This procedure may, I think, be vindicated before the tribunal of speculation.

What! Shall I, once more, knowingly and intentionally deceive myself? This procedure can by no means be justified before that strict tribunal.

I feel within me an impulse and an effort toward outward activity; this appears to be true, and to be the only truth belonging to the matter. Since it is I who feel this impulse, and since I cannot pass beyond myself, either with my whole consciousness or in particular with my capacity of sensation; since this I itself is the last point at which I am conscious of this impulse, it certainly appears to me as an impulse, founded in myself, to an activity also founded in myself. But may it not be that this impulse unknown to me is in reality the impulse of a foreign power invisible to me, and that the notion of independence is merely a delusion arising from my sphere of vision being limited to myself alone? I have no reason to assume this, but just as little reason to deny it. I must confess that I know absolutely nothing—and can know nothing—about it.

Do I then indeed feel that real *power* of free action which, strangely enough, I ascribe to myself without knowing anything of it? By no means. It is merely the *determinable* element which, by the well-known laws of thought whereby all capacities and all powers arise, we assume and add to the *determinate* element—the real action which, similarly, is only an assumption.

Is that procession—from the mere conception to an imaginary realization of it—anything more than the usual and well-known procedure of all objective thought, which seeks to shape itself, not as mere thought, but as something more? By what sophistry can this procedure be made of more value here than in any other case? Can it possess any deeper significance when to the conception of a thought it adds a realization of this thought, than when to the conception of this table it adds an actual and present table? "The conception of a purpose, a particular determination of events in me, appears in a double shape: partly as *subjective,* a thought, and partly as *objective,* an action." What reason which would not itself stand in need of a genetic deduction could I adduce against this explanation?

I say that I feel this impulse; it is therefore I myself who say so, and think so while I say it. Do I then really feel, or only think that I feel? Is not all that I call feeling only a presentation produced by my objective process of thought, and indeed the first transition-point of all objectivity? And then again, do I really think, or do I merely think that I think? And do I think that I really think, or merely that I possess the idea of thinking? What can hinder speculation from raising such questions and continuing to raise them without end? What can I answer, and where is there a point at which I can command such questionings to cease? I know, and must admit, that each definite act of consciousness may be made the subject of reflection, and a new consciousness of the first consciousness may thus be created; and that thereby the immediate consciousness is raised a step higher, and the first consciousness darkened and made doubtful; and that to this ladder there is no highest step. I know that all skepticism rests upon this process, and that the system which has so violently prostrated me is founded on the adoption and the clear consciousness of this process.

I know that if I am not merely to play another perplexing game with this system, but intend really and practically to adopt it, I must refuse obedience to that voice within me. I cannot *will* to act, for according to that system I cannot *know* whether I can really act or not. I can never believe that I truly act; that which seems to be my action must appear to me as entirely without meaning, as a mere delusive picture. All earnestness and all reality are banished from my life; and life, as well as thought, is transformed into a mere play which proceeds from nothing and tends to nothing.

Shall I then refuse obedience to that inward voice? I will not do so. I will freely accept the vocation which this impulse assigns to me, and in this resolution I will lay hold at once of thought, in all its reality and truthfulness, and on the reality of all things which are presupposed therein. I will restrict myself to the position of natural thought in which this impulse places me, and cast from me all those overrefined and sophistical inquiries which alone could make me doubtful of its truth.

I understand you now, sublime Spirit! I have found the means by which to apprehend this reality and, with this, probably all other reality. Knowledge is not this means; no knowledge can be its own foundation, its own proof; every knowledge presupposes another higher knowledge on which it is founded, and to this ascent there is no end. It is *faith, that voluntary acquiescence* in the view which is naturally presented to us, because only through this view can we fulfill our vocation. This it is which first lends a sanction to knowledge and raises to certainty and conviction that which without it might be mere delusion. It is not knowledge, but a decision of the will to allow the validity of knowledge.

Let me hold fast forever by this doctrine, which is no mere verbal distinction, but a true and deep one, bearing with it the most important consequences for my whole existence and character. All my conviction is but faith; and it proceeds from feeling, not from the understanding. Knowing this, I will enter upon no subtle disputation, because I foresee that thereby nothing can be gained; I will not suffer myself to be perplexed by it, for the source of my conviction lies higher than all disputation; I will not suffer myself to entertain the desire of pressing this conviction on others by reasoning, and I will not be surprised if such an undertaking should fail. I have adopted my mode of thinking first of all for myself, not for others, and before myself only will I justify it. He who possesses the honest, upright purpose of which I am conscious will also attain a similar conviction; without the purpose, the conviction can in no way be attained. Now that I know this, I also know from what point all cultivation of myself and others must proceed—from the will, not from the understanding. If the will is steadily and honestly directed toward the good, then the understanding will of itself apprehend the true. If the understanding is exercised only while the will remains neglected, there can arise nothing whatever but a dexterity in groping after vain and empty refinements within an absolute void. Now that I know this, I am able to confute all false knowledge that may rise in opposition to my faith. I know that every pretended truth, produced by mere speculative thought, and not founded upon faith, is assuredly false and surreptitious; for mere knowledge, thus produced, leads only to the conviction that we can know nothing. I know that such false knowledge never can discover anything but what, through faith, it has previously placed in its premises, from which it probably draws conclusions which are wholly false. Now that I know this, I possess the touchstone of all truth and of all conviction. Conscience alone is the root of all truth. Whatever is opposed to conscience or stands in the way of the fulfillment of her behests is assuredly false; I could never become convinced, even if I should be unable to discover the fallacies by which it is produced.

So has it been with all men who have ever seen the light of this world. Without being conscious of it they apprehend, through faith alone, all the reality which has an existence for them; and this faith forces itself on them simultaneously with their existence—it is born with them. How could it be otherwise? If in mere knowledge, in mere perception and reflection, there is no ground for regarding our mental presentations as more than mere pictures which necessarily pass before our view, why do we yet regard them as being *more* than this, and why do we assume, as their foundation, something which exists independently of all presentation? If we all possess the capacity and the instinct to go beyond our first natural view of things, why do so few actually go beyond it, and why do we defend ourselves, even with a sort of bitterness, from every attempt to persuade us to this course? What is it which holds us within the power of this first natural belief? Not inferences of reason, for there are none such. It is our *interest* in a reality which we desire to produce: in the good, absolutely for its own sake, and the common and sensuous, for the sake of the enjoyment they afford. No one who lives can divest himself of this interest, and just as little can he cast off the faith which this interest brings with it. We are all born in faith; he who is blind, follows blindly the secret and irresistible impulse; he who sees, follows by sight, and believes because he resolves to believe.

What unity and completeness this view presents! What dignity it confers on human nature! Our thought is not founded on itself alone, independently of our impulses and affections. Man does not consist of two independent and separate elements; he is absolutely one. All our thought is founded on our impulses; as a man's affections are, so is his knowledge. These impulses compel us to a certain mode of thought only so long as we do not perceive the constraint; the constraint vanishes the moment it is perceived; and it is then no longer the unconscious impulse, but we ourselves who form our own system of thought in accordance with it.

But I shall open my eyes, shall learn thoroughly to know myself; I shall recognize that constraint—this is my vocation. This is what I shall do; and under that supposition I shall necessarily form my own mode of thought. Then shall I stand absolutely independent, thoroughly equipped and perfected through my own act and deed. The source of all my other thoughts and even of my life itself—that from which everything proceeds which can have an existence in me, for me, or through me, the innermost spirit of my spirit—is no longer a foreign power; it is, in the strictest possible sense, my own reasonable act. I am wholly my own creation. I might have followed blindly the leading of my spiritual nature, but I resolve to be a work not of Nature but of myself, and I have become so even by means of this resolution. By endless subtleties I might have made the natural conviction of my own mind dark and doubtful, but I have accepted this conviction with freedom simply because I have resolved to accept it. With settled purpose and deliberation, I have chosen this mode of thought from among other possibilities, because I have recognized in it the only one consistent with my dignity and my vocation. With freedom and consciousness I have returned to the point at which Nature had left me. I accept that which she announces, but I accept it not because I must—I believe it because I will.

The true dignity of my understanding fills me with reverence. It is no longer the deceptive mirror which reflects a series of empty pictures, proceeding from nothing and tending to nothing; it is bestowed upon me for a great purpose. Its cultivation for this purpose is entrusted to me; it is placed in my hands, and at my hands it will be required: It is placed in my hands. I know immediately—and here my faith accepts the testimony of my consciousness without further criticism—that I am not under the necessity of allowing my thoughts to float about without direction or purpose. I know that I can voluntarily arouse and direct my attention to one object, or turn it toward another; I know that I am free continuously to investigate any object until I thoroughly understand it and feel quite satisfied about it; I know that it is neither a blind necessity which compels me to a certain mode of thought, nor an empty chance which runs riot with my thoughts; but that it is I who think, and that I can think of that whereof I choose to think. Thus by reflection I have discovered something more; I have discovered that I myself, by my own act alone, determine my whole mode of thought, and the particular view which I take of truth in general. It remains with me either to deprive myself of all sense of truth through overrefinement or to yield myself to it with faithful obedience. My whole mode of thought and the cultivation which my understanding receives, as well as the objects to which I direct it, depend entirely on myself. True insight is merit; the perversion of my capacity for knowledge, thoughtlessness, obscurity, error, and unbelief is guilt.

There is but one point toward which I have unceasingly to direct all my attention—namely, what I *ought to do* and how I may best fulfill the obligation. All my thoughts must have a bearing on my actions and must be capable of being considered as means, however remote, to this end; otherwise they are an idle and aimless show, a mere waste of time and strength, the perversion of a noble power which is entrusted to me for a very different end.

I dare hope, I dare surely promise myself, to follow out this undertaking with good results. The Nature on which I have to act is not a foreign element, called into existence without reference to me, into which I cannot penetrate. It is molded by my own laws of thought, and must be in harmony with them; it must be thoroughly transparent, knowable, and penetrable to me, even to its inmost recesses. In all its phenomena it expresses nothing but the connections and relations of my own being to myself; and as surely as I may hope to know myself, so surely may I expect to comprehend it. Let me seek only that which I ought to seek, and I shall find; let me ask only that which I ought to ask, and I shall receive an answer.

I

That voice within my soul in which I believe, and on account of which I believe everything I do believe, does not command me merely to act *in general*. This is impossible; all these general principles are formed only through my own voluntary observation and reflection applied to many individual facts, but never in themselves express any fact whatever. This voice of my conscience announces to me precisely what I ought to do, and what leave undone, in every particular situation of life; it accompanies me, if I will but listen to it with attention, through all the events of my life, and never refuses me its teaching[1] when I am called upon to act. It justifies immediate conviction, and irresistibly compels my assent to its behests; it is impossible for me to contend against it.

To listen to it, to obey it honestly and unreservedly, without fear or equivocation: this is my true vocation, the whole end and purpose of my existence. My life ceases to be an empty play without truth or significance. There is something that must absolutely be done for its own sake alone; that which conscience demands of me in this particular situation of life it is mine to do. For this only am I here: to know it, I have understanding; to perform it, I have power.

Through this edict of conscience alone, truth and reality are introduced into my conceptions. I cannot refuse them my attention and my obedience without thereby surrendering the very purposes of my existence.

Hence I cannot withhold my belief from the reality which they announce, without at the same time renouncing my vocation. It is absolutely true, without further proof or confirmation—nay, it is the first truth and the foundation of all other truth and certainty—that this voice must be obeyed. And, therefore, everything becomes to me true and certain whose truth and certainty is presupposed in the possibility of such obedience.

There appear before me in space certain phenomena to which I transfer the idea of myself; I conceive of them as beings like myself. Speculation, when carried out to its last results, has indeed taught me, or would teach me, that these supposed rational beings external to me are but the products of my own presentative power; that, according to certain laws of my thought, I am compelled to represent out of myself my conception of myself; and that, according

1 [Reading *"Belohnung"* as *"Belehrung".*]

to the same laws, I can transfer this conception only to certain definite objects. But the voice of my conscience thus speaks: "Whatever these beings may be in and for themselves, you shall act toward them as self-existent, free, substantive beings, wholly independent of yourself. Assume it, as already known, that they can give a purpose to their own being, wholly by themselves and quite independently of you; never interrupt the accomplishment of this purpose, but rather further it to the utmost of your power. Honor their freedom, take up their purposes with love as if they were your own." Thus I ought to act; by this course of action all my thought *ought* to be guided; and it will necessarily be so guided if I have resolved to obey the voice of my conscience. Hence I shall always regard these beings as in possession of an existence for themselves wholly independent of mine, as capable of forming and carrying out their own purposes; from this point of view, I shall never be able to conceive of them otherwise, and my previous speculations regarding them shall vanish like an empty dream. I *think* of them as beings like myself, I have said; but, strictly speaking, it is not by mere thought that they are first presented to me as such. It is by the voice of my conscience, by the command: "Here set a limit to your freedom; here recognize and honor purposes which are not your own." This it is which is first translated into the thought, "Here, certainly and truly, are beings like myself, free and independent." To view them otherwise, I must in action renounce, and in speculation disregard, the voice of my own conscience.

Other phenomena present themselves before me which I do not regard as beings like myself, but as things irrational. Speculation finds no difficulty in showing how the conception of such things is developed solely from my own presentative faculty and its necessary modes of activity. But I apprehend these things, also, through want, desire, and enjoyment. Not by the mental conception, but by hunger, thirst, and their satisfaction does anything become for me food and drink. I am necessitated to believe in the reality of that which threatens my sensuous existence, or in that which alone is able to maintain it. Conscience enters the field in order that it may at once sanctify and restrain this natural impulse. "You shall maintain, exercise, and strengthen yourself and your physical powers, for they have been taken account of in the plans of reason. But you can maintain them only by legitimate use, conformable to their nature. There are also, besides you, many other beings like yourself whose powers have been counted upon like your own, and can be maintained only in the same way as your own. Concede to them the same privilege that has been allowed to you. Respect what belongs to them as their possession—use what belongs to you legitimately as your own." Thus ought I to act—according to this course of action must I think. I am compelled to regard these things as standing under their own natural laws—independent of, though perceivable by, me—and, therefore, to ascribe to them an independent existence. I am compelled to believe in such laws; the task of investigating them is set before me, and that empty speculation vanishes like a mist when the genial sun appears.

In short, there is for me absolutely no such thing as an existence which has no relation to myself, and which I contemplate merely for the sake of contemplating it; whatever has an existence for me has it only through its relation to my own being. But there is, in the highest sense, only one relation to me possible, all others are but subordinate forms of this: my vocation to moral activity. My world is the object and sphere of my duties, and absolutely nothing more; there is no other world for me, and no other qualities of my world; my whole united capacity, all finite capacity, is insufficient to comprehend any other. Whatever possesses an existence for me can bring its existence and reality into contact with me only through this relation, and only through this relation do I comprehend it; for any other existence than this I have no organ whatever.

To the question, whether, in fact, such a world exists as that which I represent to myself, I can give no answer more fundamental, or evident, than this: I have, most certainly and truly, these determinate duties which announce themselves to me as duties toward certain objects, to be fulfilled by means of certain materials—duties which I cannot otherwise conceive of, and cannot otherwise fulfill, than within such a world as I represent to myself. Even to one who had never meditated on his own moral vocation, if there could be such a one, or who, if he had given it some general consideration, had never had any intention of fulfilling at any definite time in the future—even for him, his sensuous world, and his belief in its reality, arises in no other manner than from his ideas of a moral world. If he does not apprehend it by the thought of his duties, he certainly does so by the demand for his rights. What he may never require of himself, he certainly exacts from others in their conduct toward him—that they should treat him with propriety, consideration, and respect, not as an irrational thing, but as a free and independent being. And thus, by supposing in them an ability to comply with his own demands, he is compelled also to regard them as themselves considerate, free, and independent of the dominion of mere natural power. Even should he never propose to himself any other purpose in his use and enjoyment of surrounding objects but simply that of enjoying them, he at least demands this enjoyment as a right in the possession of which he claims to be left undisturbed by others; and thus he apprehends even the irrational world of sense by means of a moral idea. These claims of respect for his rationality, independence, and preservation, no one can resign who possesses a conscious existence; and with these claims, at least, there is united in his soul earnestness, renunciation of doubt, and faith in a reality, even if they be not associated with the recognition of a moral law within him. Take the man who denies his own moral vocation, as well as your existence and the existence of a material world, except as a mere futile speculation—approach him practically, apply his own principles to life and act as if either he had no existence at all or were merely a portion of rude matter; he will soon lay aside his scornful indifference, indignantly complain of you; earnestly call your attention to your conduct toward him, maintain that you should not and must not so act, and thus prove to you, by deeds, that you are assuredly capable of acting upon him; that *he is,* and that *you are,* that there is a *medium through which you can influence him,* and that you, at least, have duties to perform toward him.

Our consciousness of a reality external to ourselves is thus not rooted in the operation of supposed external objects, which indeed exist for us, and we for them, only in so far as we already know of them; nor is it an empty vision evoked by our own imagination and thought, the products of which must, like itself, be mere empty pictures; it is rather the necessary faith in our own freedom and power, in our own real activity, and in the definite laws of human action, which lies at the root of all our consciousness of a reality external to ourselves—a consciousness which is itself but faith, since it is founded on another faith, of which however it is a necessary consequence. We are compelled to believe that we act, and that we ought to act in a certain manner. We are compelled to assume a certain sphere for this action: this sphere is the real, actually present world, such as we find it—and the world is absolutely nothing more than this sphere, and cannot in any way extend beyond it. From this necessity of action proceeds the consciousness of the actual world and not the reverse way; the consciousness of the actual world is derived from the necessity of action. We act not because we know, but we know because we are called upon to act: the practical reason is

the root of all reason. The laws of action for rational beings are *immediately certain;* their world is certain only
through the fact that they are certain. We cannot deny
these laws without plunging the world, and ourselves with
it, into absolute annihilation; we raise ourselves from this
abyss and maintain ourselves above it, solely by our moral
activity.

II

There is something which I am called upon to do, simply
in order that it may be done; something to avoid doing,
solely that it may be left undone. But can I act without
having an end in view beyond the action itself, without
directing my intention toward something which can become possible by means of my action, and only by means
of it? Can I will without having something which I will?
No; this would be contradictory to the very nature of my
mind. To every action there is united in my thought, immediately and by the laws of thought itself, a condition of
future things, to which my action is related as cause to
effect. But this purpose or end of my action must not be
proposed to me for its own sake through some necessity,
say of Nature, and my course of action then determined
according to this end; I must not have an end assigned
to me, and then inquire how I must act in order to attain
this end; my action must not be dependent on the end: I
must act in a certain manner simply because I ought so
to act—this is the first point. That a result will follow
from this course of action is proclaimed by the voice
within me. This result necessarily becomes an end to me,
since I am bound to perform the action that brings it,
and it alone, to pass. I will that something shall come to
pass, because I must act so that it may come to pass. I am
hungry not because food is before me, but a thing becomes

food for me because I am hungry; similarly, I act as I do
not because a certain end is to be attained, but the end
becomes an end to me because I am bound to act in the
manner by which it may be attained. I do not first view the
point toward which I am to draw my line, and then, by its
position, determine the direction of my line and the angle
it shall make; rather I draw my line absolutely in a right
angle, and thereby the points are determined through
which my line must pass. The end does not determine the
commandment; on the contrary, the immediately given pur-
port of the commandment determines the end.

I say it is the commandment to act that of itself assigns
an end to my action—the same inward power that compels
me to think that I ought to act thus compels me also to
believe that from my action some result will arise; it opens
to my spiritual vision a prospect into another world, which
is indeed a world, a condition, and not an action, but
another and better world than that which is present to the
physical eye. It constrains me to aspire after this better
world, to embrace it with every power, to long for its realization, to live only in it, and in it alone find satisfaction.
The commandment is my guarantee for the certain attainment of this end. The same resolution by which I devote
my whole thought and life to the fulfillment of this law,
and determine to see nothing beyond it, brings with it the
indestructible conviction that the promise it implies is likewise true and certain, and renders it impossible for me
even to conceive the possibility of the opposite. As I live
in obedience to it, so do I live also in the contemplation of
its end—in that better world which it promises to me.

Even in the mere consideration of the world as it is, apart
from this law, there arises within me the wish, the desire—
no, not the mere desire, but the absolute demand—for a
better world. I cast a glance on the present relations of

men toward each other and toward Nature: on the feeble-
ness of their powers, on the strength of their desires and
passions. A voice within me proclaims with irresistible conviction: "It is impossible that it can remain thus; it must
become other and better."

I cannot think of the present state of humanity as that
in which it is destined to remain; I am unable to conceive
of this as its complete and final vocation. Then, indeed,
were all a dream and a delusion; and it would not be worth
the trouble to have lived and played out this ever-repeated
game which tends to nothing and signifies nothing. Only
in so far as I can regard this condition as the means toward
a better, as the transition point to a higher and more perfect, condition has it any value in my eyes. I can support
it, esteem it, and joyfully perform my part in it, not for its
own sake, but for the sake of that better world for which it
prepares the way. My soul can accept no place in the present, nor rest in it even for a moment; my whole being flows
onward, incessantly and irresistibly, toward that future and
better state of things.

Shall I eat and drink only that I may be hungry and
thirsty, and eat and drink again, till the grave which is open
beneath my feet shall swallow me up and I myself become
the food of worms? Shall I beget beings like myself, that
they too may eat and drink and die, and leave behind them
beings like themselves to do over again the same things
that I have done? To what purpose this ever-revolving
circle, this ceaseless and unvarying round, in which all
things appear only to pass away, and pass away only that
they may reappear as they were before—this monster continually devouring itself that it may again bring itself forth,
and bringing itself forth only that it may again devour
itself?

This can never be the vocation of my being, or of all
being. There must be something which exists because it has
come into existence, and endures and, having once become

such as it is, cannot come anew. This abiding existence must be produced amid the vicissitudes of the transitory and perishable, maintain itself there, and be borne onward, pure and inviolate, upon the waves of time.

Our species still laboriously extorts the means of its subsistence and preservation from an opposing Nature. The larger portion of mankind is still condemned through life to severe toil in order to supply nourishment for itself and for the smaller portion which thinks for it; immortal spirits are compelled to fix their whole thoughts and endeavors on the earth that brings forth their food. It still frequently happens that, when the laborer has completed his toil and has promised himself in return a lasting endurance for himself and for his work, a hostile element will destroy in a moment that which it has cost him years of patient forethought and industry to accomplish, and the assiduous and careful man is undeservedly made the prey of hunger and misery; often do floods, storms, volcanoes desolate whole countries, and works which bear the impress of a rational soul are mingled with their authors in the wild chaos of destruction and death. Disease sweeps into an untimely grave men in the pride of their strength and children whose existence has yet borne no fruit; pestilence stalks through blooming lands, leaves the few who escape its ravages like lonely orphans bereaved of the accustomed support of their fellows, and does all that it can do to give back to the wilderness regions which the labor of man has reclaimed from thence as a possession to himself. Thus it is now, but thus it cannot remain forever. No work that bears the stamp of Reason, and has been undertaken to extend her power, can ever be wholly lost in the onward progress of the ages. The sacrifices which the irregular violence of Nature extorts from Reason must at last exhaust, satiate, and appease that violence. The same power which has burst out into lawless fury cannot again commit like excesses; it cannot be destined to renew its ravages; by its own outbreak its energies must henceforth and forever be exhausted. All those outbreaks of unregulated power before which human strength vanishes into nothing, those desolating hurricanes, those earthquakes, those volcanoes can be nothing but the last struggles of the rude mass against the law of regular, progressive, living, and systematic activity to which it is compelled to submit in opposition to its own undirected impulses—nothing but the last shivering strokes by which the perfect formation of our globe has yet to be accomplished. The resistance must gradually become weaker and at length be worn out, since, in the regulated progress of things, there can be nothing to renew its strength; that formation must at length be achieved and our destined dwelling place be made complete. Nature must gradually be resolved into a condition in which her regular action may be calculated and safely relied upon, and her power bear a fixed and definite relation to that which is destined to govern it—that of man. In so far as this relation already exists and the cultivation of Nature has attained a firm footing, the works of man, by their mere existence and by an influence altogether beyond the original intent of their authors, shall again react upon Nature and become to her a new vivifying principle. Cultivation shall quicken and ameliorate the sluggish and baleful atmosphere of primeval forests, deserts, and marshes; more regular and varied cultivation shall diffuse throughout the air new impulses to life and fertility; and the sun shall pour his animating rays into an atmosphere breathed by healthful, industrious, and civilized nations. Science, first called into existence by the pressure of necessity, shall afterwards calmly and deliberately investigate the unchangeable laws of Nature, review its powers at large, and learn to calculate their possible manifestations; and, while closely following the footsteps of Nature in the living and actual world, form for itself in thought a new ideal one. Every discovery that Reason has extorted from Nature shall be maintained throughout the ages and become the ground of new knowledge for the common possession of our species. Thus shall Nature ever become more and more intelligible and transparent, even in her most secret depths; human power, enlightened and armed by human invention, shall rule over her without difficulty, and the conquest, once made, shall be peacefully maintained. This dominion of man over Nature shall gradually be extended until, at length, no further expenditure of mechanical labor shall be necessary than what the human body requires for its development, cultivation, and health; and this labor shall cease to be a burden; for a reasonable being is not destined to be a bearer of burdens.

But it is not Nature, it is Freedom itself, by which the greatest and most terrible disorders incident to our race are produced; man is the cruelest enemy of man. Lawless hordes of savages still wander over vast wildernesses—they meet, and the victor devours his foe at the triumphal feast; or where culture has at length united these wild hordes under some social bond, they attack each other, as nations, with the power which law and union have given them. Defying toil and privation, their armies traverse peaceful plains and forests; they meet each other, and the sight of their brethren is the signal for slaughter. Equipped with the mightiest inventions of the human intellect, hostile fleets plow their way through the ocean; through storm and tempest man rushes to meet his fellow men upon the lonely inhospitable sea; they meet, and defy the fury of the elements that they may destroy each other with their own hands. Even in the interior of states, where men seem to be united in equality under the law, it is still for the most part only force and fraud which rule under that venerable name; and here the warfare is so much the more shameful that it is not openly declared to be war, and the party attacked is even deprived of the privilege of defending itself against unjust oppression. Combinations of the few rejoice aloud in the ignorance, the folly, the vice, and the misery in which the greater number of their fellow men are sunk, avowedly seek to retain them in this state of degradation, and even to plunge them deeper in it in order to perpetuate their slavery—nay, would destroy anyone who should venture to enlighten or improve them. No attempt at amelioration can anywhere be made without rousing up from slumber a host of selfish interests to war against it, and uniting even the most varied and opposite in a common hostility. The good cause is ever the weaker, for it is simple and can be loved only for itself. Evil attracts each individual by the promise which is most seductive to him; and its adherents, always at war among themselves, so soon as the good makes its appearance, conclude a truce that they may unite the whole powers of their wickedness against it. Scarcely, indeed, is such an opposition needed, for even the good themselves are but too often divided by misunderstanding, error, distrust, and secret self-love, and that so much the more violently, the more earnestly each strives to propagate that which he deems to be the best; and thus internal discord dissipates a power which, even when united, could scarcely hold the balance with evil. One blames the other for rushing onward with stormy impetuosity to his object, without waiting until the way shall have been prepared. He in turn is then blamed that, through hesitation and cowardice, he accomplishes nothing, but allows all things to remain as they are, contrary to his better conviction, because for him the hour of action never arrives. Only the Omniscient can determine whether either of the parties in the dispute is in the right. Everyone regards that undertaking the necessity of which is most apparent to him, and for the prosecution of which he has acquired the greatest skill, as most important and needful—as the point from which all improvement must proceed. Each man requires all good men to unite their efforts with his, and to subject themselves to him for the accomplishment of his particular purpose, holding it to be treason to the good cause if they hold back; while they on the other hand make the same demands upon him and accuse him of similar treason for a similar refusal. Thus do all good intentions among men appear to be lost in vain disputations, which leave behind them no trace of their existence, while in the meantime the world goes on as well, or as ill, as it can without human effort—by the blind mechanism of Nature—and so will go on forever.

And so go on forever? No! unless the whole existence of humanity is to be an idle game, without significance and without end. It cannot be intended that those savage tribes should always remain savage; no race can be born with all the capacities of perfect humanity and yet be destined never to develop these capacities, never to become more than that which a sagacious animal by its own proper nature might become. Those savages must be destined to be the progenitors of more powerful, cultivated, and virtuous generations; otherwise it is impossible to conceive of a purpose in their existence, or even of the possibility of their existence in a world ordered and arranged by reason. Savage races may become civilized, for this has already occurred; the most cultivated nations of modern times are the descendants of savages. Whether civilization is a direct and natural development of human society, or whether it is invariably brought about through instruction and outside example, with superhuman guidance as the primary source of all human culture—in whatever way nations which once were savage have emerged into civilization, those who are yet uncivilized will gradually attain it. They must, no doubt, at first pass through the same dangers and corruptions of a merely sensuous civilization by which the civilized nations are still oppressed, but they will thereby be brought into union with the great whole of humanity and be made capable of taking part in its further progress.

It is the vocation of our species to unite itself into one single body, all the parts of which shall be thoroughly known to each other, and all possessed of similar culture. Nature and even the passions and vices of men have from the beginning tended toward this end; a great part of the way toward it is already passed, and we may surely calculate that this end, which is the condition of all further progress, will in time be attained. Let us not ask of history if man, on the whole, has yet become purely moral! To a more extended, comprehensive, and powerful freedom he has certainly attained; but hitherto it has been an almost necessary result of his position that this choice has been applied chiefly to evil purposes. Neither let us ask whether the aesthetic and intellectual culture of the ancient world, concentrated on a few points, may not have excelled in degree that of modern times! It might happen that we should receive a humiliating answer, and that in this respect the human race has not advanced, but rather seemed to retrograde, in its riper years. But let us ask of history at what period the existing culture has been most widely diffused and distributed among the greatest number of individuals, and we shall doubtless find that, from the beginning of history down to our own day, the few landmarks of civilization have extended themselves abroad from their center, that one individual after another, and one nation after another, has been embraced within their circle, and that this wider outspread of culture is proceeding under our own eyes. And this is the first point to be attained in the endless path on which humanity must advance. Until this shall have been attained, until the existing culture of every age shall have been diffused over the whole inhabited globe and our species become capable of the most unlimited intercommunication with itself, one nation or one continent must pause on the great common path of progress and wait for the advance of the others; and each must bring as an offering to the universal commonwealth, for the sake of which alone it exists, its ages of apparent immobility or retrogression. When that first point shall have been attained, when every useful discovery made at one end of the earth shall be at once made known and communicated to all the rest, then, without further interruption, without halt or regress, with united strength and equal step, humanity shall move onward to a higher culture of which we can at present form no conception.

Within those singular associations, thrown together by unreasoning accident, which we call States—after they have subsisted for a time in peace: when the resistance excited by yet new oppression has been lulled to sleep and the fermentation of contending forces appeased, abuse, by its continuance and by general sufferance, assumes a sort of established form; and the ruling classes, in the uncontested enjoyment of their extorted privileges, have nothing more to do but to extend them further and to give to this extension also the same established form. Urged by their insatiable desires, they will continue from generation to generation their efforts to acquire wider and yet wider privileges, and never say, "It is enough!" At last oppression shall reach its limit and become wholly insupportable, and despair give back to the oppressed that power which their courage, extinguished by centuries of tyranny, could not procure for them. They will then no longer endure any among them who cannot be satisfied to stand and to abide on an equality with others. In order to protect themselves against internal violence or new oppression, all will take on themselves the same obligations. Their deliberations, in which, whatever a man may decide, he decides for himself, and not for one subject to him and whose sufferings will never affect him and in whose fate he takes no concern—deliberations, according to which no one can hope that it shall be he who is to *practice* a permitted injustice, but everyone must fear that he may have to *suffer* it—deliberations that alone deserve the name of legislation, which is something wholly different from the ordinances of combined lords to the countless herds of their slaves—these deliberations will necessarily be guided by justice, and will lay the foundation of a true state, in which each individual, from a regard for his own security, will be irresistibly compelled to respect the security of every other without exception; since, under the supposed legislation, every injury which he should attempt to do another would not fall upon its object but would infallibly recoil upon himself.

By the establishment of this only true state, this firm foundation of internal peace, the possibility of foreign war, at least with other true states, is cut off. In a true state, injury to a citizen of a neighboring state will be forbidden as strictly, and prevented as carefully, as injury to a citizen of its own, and it will call forth the same compensation and punishment. The state will so act for its own sake—to prevent the thought of injustice, plunder, and violence entering the minds of its own citizens, and to leave them no possibility of gain except by means of industry and diligence within their legitimate sphere of activity. This law concerning the security of neighbors is necessarily a law in every state that is not a robber state; and by its operation the possibility of any just complaint of one state against another, and consequently every case of self-defense among nations, is entirely prevented. There are no necessary, permanent, and immediate relations of states, as such, with each other, which should be productive of strife; there are, as a rule, only relations of the individual citizens of one state to the individual citizens of another. A state can be injured only in the person of one of its citizens, but such injury will be immediately compensated, and the aggrieved state satisfied. Between states such as these, there is no rank which can be insulted, no ambition which can be offended. No officer of one state is authorized to intermeddle in the internal affairs of another, nor is there any temptation for him to do so, since he could not derive the slightest personal advantage from any such influence. That a whole nation should determine, for the sake of plunder, to make war on a neighboring country is impossible; for in a state where all are equal, the plunder could not become the booty of a few, but must be equally divided amongst all, and the share of no one individual could ever recompense him for the trouble of the war. Only where the advantage falls to the few oppressors, and the injury, the toil, the expense to the countless herd of slaves, is a war of spoliation possible and conceivable. States such as these do not need to fear war from states like themselves. War is to be feared only from savages or barbarians whose lack of skill to enrich themselves by industry impels them to plunder, or from enslaved nations driven by their masters to a war from which they themselves will reap no advantage. In relation to the first of these dangers, every civilized state already has superior strength because of the arts of civilization; against the latter danger, the common advantage of all demands that they should strengthen themselves by union. No free state can reasonably suffer in its vicinity associations governed by rulers whose interests would be promoted by the subjugation of adjacent nations, and whose very existence is therefore a constant source of danger to their neighbors. A regard for their own security compels all free states to transform all around them into free states like themselves, and thus, for the sake of their own welfare, to extend the empire of culture over barbarism, of freedom over slavery. Soon will the nations civilized or enfranchised by them find themselves placed in the same relation toward others still enthralled by barbarism or slavery in which the earlier free nations formerly stood toward them, and be compelled to do the same things for these which were formerly done for themselves; and thus, of necessity, by reason of the existence of some few really free states will the empire of civilization, freedom, and with it universal peace, gradually embrace the whole world.

Thus, from the establishment of a just internal organization and of peace between individuals, there will necessarily result integrity in the external relations of nations toward each other, and universal peace among them. But the establishment of this just internal organization, and the emancipation of the first nation that shall be truly free, arises as a necessary consequence from the ever-growing oppression exercised by the ruling classes toward their subjects, which gradually becomes insupportable—a progress which may be safely left to the passions and the blindness of those classes, even although warned of the result.

In this sole true state, there will be no temptation to evil—not even the possibility of resolving upon an evil deed with any reasonable hope of benefit. The strongest possible inducements will be offered to every man to make virtue the sole object of his life.

There is no man who loves evil because it is evil; it is only the advantages and enjoyments expected from it—and which, in the present condition of humanity, do actually, in most cases, result from it—that are loved. So long as this condition shall continue, so long as a premium shall be set upon vice, a fundamental improvement of mankind, as a whole, can scarcely be hoped for. But in a civil society constituted as it ought to be, as reason requires it to be, as the thinker may easily describe it to himself although he may nowhere find it actually existing at the present day, but as it must necessarily exist in the first nation that shall really acquire true freedom—in such a state of society evil will present no advantages, but rather the most certain disadvantages; and self-love itself will restrain the excess of self-love when it would run out into injustice. By the unerring administration of such a state every fraud or oppression practiced upon others, all self-aggrandizement at their expense, will be rendered vain, and all labor so applied fruitless; moreover, such attempts would even recoil upon their author and assuredly bring home to himself the evil which he would cause to others. He will be punished for every injury he inflicts, whether in his own land or outside of his own land, no matter where in the whole world it may be. But it is not to be expected, even of a bad man, that he would decide upon evil merely for the sake of such a decision if he had no power to carry it into effect and if nothing could arise from it but infamy to himself. The use of liberty for evil purposes is thus destroyed; man must resolve either to renounce his freedom altogether, and patiently to become a mere passive wheel in the great machine of the universe, or else to employ it for good. In soil thus prepared good will easily prosper. When men shall no longer be divided by selfish purposes, nor their powers exhausted in struggles with each other, nothing will remain for them but to direct their united strength against the one common enemy which still remains unsubdued—resisting, uncultivated Nature. No longer estranged from each other by private ends, they will necessarily combine for this common object; and thus there arises a body everywhere animated by the same spirit and the same love. Every misfortune to the individual, since it can no longer be a gain to any other individual, is a misfortune to the whole and to each individual member of the whole; and is felt with the same pain, and remedied with the same activity, by every member; every step in advance made by one man is a step in advance made by the whole race. Here, where the petty, narrow self of mere individual personality is lost in the more comprehensive unity of the social constitution, each man truly loves every other as himself—as a member of this greater *self* which now claims all his love, and of which he himself is no more than a member, capable of participating only in a common gain or in a common loss. The strife of evil against good is here abolished, for here no evil can intrude. The strife of the good among themselves for the sake of good disappears now that they find it easy to love good for its own sake alone and not because they are its authors; now that it has become all-important to them that the truth should really be discovered, that the useful action should be done—no matter who may be the one who accomplishes it. Here each individual is at all times ready to join his strength to that of others, to make it subordinate to that of others; and whoever is acknowledged by all as most capable of accomplishing the greatest amount of good will be supported by all, and his success rejoiced in by all.

This is the purpose of earthly life, which Reason sets before us, and for the infallible attainment of which she is our pledge and security. It is not a goal which is given to us only that we may strive after it for the mere purpose of exercising our powers on something great, the real existence of which we may perhaps be compelled to abandon to doubt —it shall, it must be realized; there must be a time in which it shall be accomplished, as surely as there is a sensible world and a species of reasonable beings existent in time with respect to which nothing earnest and rational is conceivable besides this purpose, and whose existence becomes intelligible only through this purpose. Unless all human life be metamorphosed into a mere theatrical display for the gratification of some malignant spirit, who has implanted in poor humanity this inextinguishable longing for the imperishable only to amuse himself with its ceaseless pursuit of that which it can never overtake, with its ever-repeated efforts to embrace that which still eludes its grasp, with its restless hurrying on in an ever-recurring circle—only to mock its earnest aspirations with an empty, insipid farce; unless the wise man, seeing through this mockery, and feeling an irrepressible disgust at continuing to play his part in it, is to cast life indignantly from him and make the moment

of his awakening to reason also that of his physical death—
unless these things are so, this purpose most assuredly must
be attained. Yes! it is attainable *in life,* and *through life,* for
Reason commands me to live: it is attainable, for *I am.*

III

But when this end shall have been attained and humanity shall at length stand at this point, what is there then
to do? Upon earth there is no higher state than this; the
generation which has once reached it can do no more than
abide there, steadfastly maintain its position, die, and leave
behind it descendants who shall do the like, and who will
again leave behind them descendants to follow in their footsteps. Humanity would thus stand still upon her path; and
therefore her earthly end cannot be her highest end. This
earthly end is conceivable, attainable, and finite. Even
though we consider all preceding generations as means for
the attainment of the final complete one, we do not thereby
escape the question of earnest reason; to what end then
is this final generation? Since a human race has appeared
upon earth, its existence here must certainly be in accordance with, and not contrary to, reason; and it must attain all the development which it is possible for it to attain
on earth. But why should such a race have an existence at
all—why may it not as well have remained in the womb of
nothingness? Reason is not for the sake of existence, but
existence for the sake of Reason. An existence which does
not of itself satisfy Reason and solve all her questions cannot possibly be the true being.

And, then, are those actions which are commanded by
the voice of conscience—by that voice whose dictates I never
dare to criticize, but must always obey in silence—are those
actions, in reality, always the means, and the only means,

for the attainment of the earthly purpose of humanity? That I cannot do otherwise than refer them to this purpose, and dare not have any other object for them, is incontestable. But then are these my intentions always fulfilled? Is it enough that we will what is good, in order that it may happen? Alas! many virtuous resolutions are entirely lost for this world, and others appear even to hinder the purpose which they were designed to promote. On the other hand, the most despicable passions of men, even their vices and their crimes, often forward more certainly the good cause than the endeavors of the virtuous man who will never do evil that good may come! It seems that the Highest Good of the world pursues its course of increase and prosperity independently of all human virtues or vices, according to its own laws, through an invisible and unknown Power, just as the heavenly bodies run their appointed course independently of all human effort, and that this Power carries along with it, in its own great plan, all human intentions good and bad, and, with overruling wisdom, employs for its own purpose that which was undertaken for other ends.

Thus, even if the attainment of this earthly end could be the purpose of our existence, and if reason could answer every question about it, yet this end would not be ours, but the end of that unknown Power. We do not know at any given moment what is most conducive to this end; and nothing is left to us but to give by our actions some material, no matter what, for this Power to work upon, and to leave to it the task of elaborating this material to its own purposes. It would, in that case, be our highest wisdom not to trouble ourselves about matters that do not concern us; to live according to our own fancy or inclinations, and quietly leave the consequences to that unknown Power. The moral law within us would be void and superfluous, and absolutely unfitted to a being destined to nothing higher than this. In order to be at one with ourselves, we should have to refuse obedience to that law, and to suppress it as a perverse and foolish fanaticism.

No! I will not refuse obedience to the law of duty; as surely as I live and am, I will obey precisely because it commands. This resolution shall be first and highest in my mind; that to which everything else must conform, but which is itself dependent on nothing else; this shall be the innermost principle of my spiritual life.

But, as a reasonable being, before whom a purpose must be set solely by its own will and determination, I cannot act without a motive and without an end. If this obedience is to be recognized by me as a reasonable service, if the voice which demands this obedience be really that of the creative reason within me, and not a mere fanciful enthusiasm invented by my own imagination or communicated to me somehow from without, then this obedience must have some consequences and must serve some end. It is evident that it does not serve the purpose of the world of sense; hence there must be a supersensual world whose purposes it does serve.

The mist of delusion clears away from before my sight! I receive a new organ, and a new world opens before me. It is disclosed to me only by the law of reason, and answers only to that law in my spirit. I apprehend this world—limited as I am by my sensuous view I must thus name the unnamable—I apprehend this world merely in and through the end which my obedience demands; it is in reality nothing else than this necessary end itself which reason annexes to the law of duty. Setting aside everything else, how could I suppose that this law had reference to the world of sense, or that the whole end and object of the obedience which it demands is to be found within that world, since that in which alone this obedience consists serves no purpose whatever in that world, can never become a cause in it, and can never produce results. In the world of sense, which proceeds on a chain of material causes and effects, and in which whatever happens depends merely on that which preceded it, it is never of any moment *how and with what motives and intentions* an action is performed, but only *what the action is.*

Had it been the sole purpose of our existence to produce an earthly condition of our race, there would have been required only an unerring mechanism by which our outward actions might have been determined—we need have been no more than wheels well fitted to the great machine. Freedom would have been not merely vain, but even obstructive; a virtuous will wholly superfluous. The world would, in that case, have been most unskillfully directed, and attain the purposes of its existence by wasteful extravagance and circuitous by-ways. Had you, mighty World-Spirit, withheld from us this freedom which you are now constrained to adapt to your plans with labor and contrivance; had you rather at once compelled us to act in the way in which your plans required that we should act, you would have attained your purposes by a much shorter way, as the humblest of the dwellers in this your world can tell you. But I am free; and therefore such a chain of causes and effects, in which freedom is absolutely superfluous and without aim, cannot exhaust my whole nature. I must be free; for that which constitutes our true worth is not the mere mechanical act, but the free determination of free will, for the sake of duty and for the ends of duty only— thus speaks the voice of conscience within us. The bond with which this law of duty binds me is a bond for living spirits only; it disdains to rule over a dead mechanism and addresses its decrees only to the living and the free. It requires of me this obedience—this obedience cannot be superfluous.

And now the Eternal World rises before me more brightly, and the fundamental law of its order stands clearly and distinctly apparent to my mental vision. In this world, *will* alone, as it lies concealed from mortal eye in the secret obscurities of the soul, is the first link in a chain of consequences that stretches through the whole invisible realms of spirit, as, in the physical world, *action*—a certain movement of matter—is the first link in a material chain that runs through the whole system of Nature. The will is the efficient, living principle of the world of reason, as motion is the efficient, living principle of the world of sense. I stand in the center of two entirely opposite worlds: a visible world, in which action is the only moving power; and an invisible and absolutely incomprehensible world, in which will is the ruling principle. I am one of the primitive forces of both these worlds. My will embraces both. This will is, in itself, a constituent element of the supersensual world; for as I move my will by successive resolutions I move and change something in that world, throughout which my activity thus extends itself giving birth to new and ever-enduring results which henceforward possess a real existence and need not be again produced. This will may break forth in a material act; and this act belongs to the world of sense and does there what it can do.

It is not necessary that I should first be severed from the terrestrial world before I can obtain admission into the world beyond the earth; I am and live in it even now, far more truly than in the terrestrial; even now it is my only sure foundation, and the eternal life on the possession of which I have already entered is the only ground why I should still prolong this earthly one. That which we call heaven does not lie beyond the grave; it is even here diffused around us, and its light arises in every pure heart. My will is mine, and it is the only thing that is wholly mine and entirely dependent on myself; and through it I have already become a citizen of the realm of freedom and of pure spiritual activity. What determination of my will—of the only thing by which I am raised from earth into this region—is best adapted to the order of the spiritual world is proclaimed to me at every moment by my conscience, the bond that constantly unites me to the spiritual world; it depends solely on myself to give my activity the appointed direction. Thus I cultivate myself for this world, labor in it and for it, in cultivating one of its members; in it, and only in it, I pursue my purpose according to a settled plan, without doubt or hesitation, certain of the result, since here no foreign power stands opposed to my free will. That in the world of sense my will, truly so called, also becomes an action is but the law of this sensuous world. I did not send forth the act as I did the will; only the latter was wholly and purely my work—it was all that proceeded forth from me. It was not even necessary that there should be another particular act on my part to unite the deed to the will; the deed unites itself to it according to the law of that second world with which I am connected through my will, and in which this will is likewise an original force, as it is in the first. When I regard my will, determined according to the dictates of conscience, as a fact and an efficient cause in the world of sense, I am indeed compelled to refer it to that earthly purpose of humanity as a means to the accomplishment of an end. But I do not first survey the plan of the world and from this knowledge calculate what I have to do; rather the specific action which conscience directly enjoins me to do reveals itself to me at once as the only means by which, in my position, I can contribute to the attainment of that end. Even if it should afterwards appear as if this end had not been promoted—nay, if it should even seem to have been hindered—by my action, yet I can never regret it, nor perplex myself about it, so surely as I have truly obeyed my conscience in performing this act. Whatever consequences it may have in this world, in the other world there can nothing but good result from it. And even in this world, should my action appear to have failed of its purpose, my conscience *for that very reason* commands me to repeat it in a manner by which it may more effectually reach its end; or, should the action seem to have hindered that purpose, my conscience *for that very reason* commands me to make good the detriment and annihilate the untoward result. I will as I *ought*, and the new deed follows. It may happen that the consequences of this new action, in the world of sense, may appear to me not more beneficial than those of the first; but with respect to the other world I retain the same calm assurance as before; and in the present it is again my bounden duty to make good my previous failure by new action. And thus should it still appear that, during my whole earthly life, I have not advanced the good cause a single hair's breadth in this world, yet I dare not cease my efforts: after every unsuccessful attempt I must still believe that the next will be successful. But in the spiritual world no step is ever lost. In short, I pursue the earthly purpose not for its own sake alone or as a final aim, but only because my true final aim, obedience to the law of conscience, does not present itself to me in this world in any other shape than as the advancement of this end. I may not cease to pursue it unless I were to deny the law of duty, or unless that law were to manifest itself to me, in this life, in some other shape than as a commandment to promote this purpose in my own place; I shall actually cease to pursue it in another life in which that commandment shall have set before me some other purpose wholly incomprehensible to me here. In this life, I must *will* to promote it, because I must obey; whether it be *actually* promoted by the deed that follows my will thus fittingly directed is not my concern: I am responsible only for the *will* (which indeed in the world of sense can have to do only with the earthly purpose), but not for the result. Previous to the actual deed I can never resign this purpose; the deed, when it is completed, I may resign and repeat it or improve it. Thus do I live and labor, even here, in my most essential nature and in my nearest purposes, only for the other world; and my activity for it is the only thing of which I am completely certain. In the world of sense I labor only for the sake of the other, and only because I cannot work for the other without at least *willing* to work for the world of sense.

I will establish myself firmly in this, to me, wholly new view of my vocation. The present life cannot be rationally regarded as the sole purpose of my existence or of the existence of a human race in general; there is something in me, and there is something required of me, which finds in this life nothing to which it can be applied, and which is entirely superfluous and unnecessary for the attainment of the highest objects that can be attained on earth. There must therefore be a purpose in human existence which lies beyond this life. But should the present life, which is nevertheless imposed upon us, and which may possibly be designed solely for the development of reason—since even awakened reason commands us to maintain it and to promote its highest purposes with all our powers—should this life not prove entirely vain and ineffectual, it must at least have relation to a future life, as means to an end. Now there is nothing in this present life, the ultimate consequences of which do not remain on earth—nothing whereby we could be connected with a future life except by our virtuous will, which in this world, by the fundamental laws thereof, is in itself entirely fruitless. Only by means of our virtuous will can we labor for another life, and for the first and nearest objects which are there revealed to us; and it is through the consequences, invisible to us, of this virtuous will that we first acquire a firm standing point in that other life, whence we may then advance in a further course of progress.

That our virtuous will in and for and through itself must have consequences, we know already in this life, for reason cannot command anything which is without a purpose; but *what* these consequences may be, nay, how it is even possible for a mere will to produce any effect at all— as to this we can form no conception whatever so long as we are still involved in this material world; and it is true wisdom not to undertake an inquiry in which we know beforehand that we cannot be successful. With respect to the nature of these consequences, the present life is therefore, in relation to the future, *a life in faith.* In the future life, we shall possess these consequences, for we shall then proceed from them as our starting point and build upon them as our foundation; and this other life will thus be, in relation to the consequences of our virtuous will in the present, *a life present to our sight.* In that other life, we shall also have an immediate purpose set before us, as we have in the present; for our activity must not cease. But we remain finite beings; and for finite beings there is but finite, determinate activity; and every determinate act has a determinate end. In the present life, the adjustment of this world to the work we have to do, the degree of culture and virtue already attained by men, and our own physical powers are related to the purposes of this life; in the future life, the consequences of our virtuous will in the present shall stand in the same relation to the purposes of that other existence. The present is the beginning of our existence; the endowments requisite for its purpose, and a firm footing in it, have been freely bestowed on us. The future is the continuation of this existence, and in it we must acquire for ourselves a beginning, and a definite standing point.

And now the present life no longer appears vain and useless. For this and this alone it is given to us: that we may acquire for ourselves a firm foundation in the future life, and only by means of this foundation is this present life connected with our whole existence. It is very possible that, as in the present life, our finite powers will not be able to attain the immediate purposes of this second life with certainty or in accord with a fixed plan; and that even there a virtuous will may appear superfluous and without result. But it can never be lost there, any more than here, for it is the eternal and unalterable command of reason. Its necessary efficacy would, in that case, direct us to a third life, in which the consequences of our virtuous will in the second life would become visible—a life which during the second life would again be believed in through faith, but with firmer, more unwavering confidence, since we should already have had practical experience of the truthfulness of reason, and have regained the fruits of a pure heart which had been faithfully garnered up in a previously completed life.

As in the present life, it is only from the command of conscience to follow a certain course of action that there arises our conception of a certain purpose in this action, and from this our whole intuitive perception of a world of sense; so, in the future, upon a similar, but now to us wholly inconceivable command, will be founded our conception of the immediate purpose of that life; and upon this, again, our intuitive perception of a world in which we shall set out from the consequences of our virtuous will in the present life. The present world exists for us only through the law of duty; the other will be revealed to us, in a similar manner, through another command of duty; for in no other manner can a world exist for any reasonable being.

This, then, is my whole sublime vocation, my true nature. I am a member of two orders: the one purely spiritual, in which I rule by my will alone; the other sensuous, in which I operate by my deed. The sole end of reason is pure activity, absolutely by itself alone, having no need of any instrument outside of itself—independent of everything which is not reason, absolutely unconditioned. The will is the living principle of reason—is itself reason, when purely and simply apprehended. That reason is active by itself alone—this means that pure will, merely as such, lives and rules. It is only the Infinite Reason that lives immediately and wholly in this purely spiritual order. The finite reason—which does not of itself constitute the world of reason, but is only one of its many members—lives necessarily at the same time in a sensuous order; that is to say, in one which presents to it an end other than the pure activity of reason: a material goal to be promoted by instruments and powers which indeed stand under the immediate dominion of the will, but whose activity is also conditioned by their own natural laws. Yet, as surely as reason is reason, the will must operate absolutely by itself and independently of the natural laws by which the material action is determined; and hence the sensuous life of every finite being points toward a higher life, into which the will, by itself alone, may open the way, and of which it may acquire possession—a possession which indeed we are again constrained to conceive of sensuously as a state, and not as a mere will.

These two orders—the purely spiritual and the sensuous, the latter consisting possibly of an innumerable series of particular lives—have existed for me since the first moment of the development of an active reason within me, and still continue parallel to each other. The latter order is only a phenomenon for myself, and for those with whom I am associated in this life; the former alone gives it significance, purpose, and value. I *am* immortal, imperishable, eternal, as soon as I form the resolution to obey the laws of reason; I do not need to *become* so. The supersensual world is no future world; it is now present; it can at no point of finite existence be more present than at another; not more present after an existence of myriads of lives than at this moment. My sensuous existence may, in the future, assume other forms, but these will be just as little the true life as is its present form. By that resolution I lay hold on eternity, and cast off this earthly life and all other forms of sensuous life which may yet lie before me, and place myself far above them. I become the sole source of my own being and its phenomena, and, henceforth, unconditioned by anything without me, I have life in myself. My will, directed by no foreign agency in the order of the supersensual world but by myself alone, is this source of true life, and of eternity.

But it is my will alone which is this source of true life and of eternity: only by recognizing this will as the true seat of moral goodness, and by actually raising it thereto, do I obtain the assurance and the possession of that supersensual world.

Without regard to any conceivable or visible object, without inquiry as to whether my will may be followed by any result other than the mere volition, I must will in accordance with the moral law. My will stands alone, apart from all that is not itself, and is its own world merely by itself and for itself; not only as being itself an absolutely *first,* primary and original, power, before which there is no preceding influence by which it may be governed, but also as being followed by no conceivable or comprehensible *second* step in the series, by which its activity may be brought under the dominion of a foreign law. If there were to proceed from it any second result, and from this again a third result, and so on, in any conceivable sensuous world distinct from the spiritual world, then its strength would be broken by the resistance of the independent elements which such a world would set in motion; the mode of its activity would no longer exactly correspond to the purpose expressed in the volition; and the will would be no longer free, but be in so far limited by the laws of its heterogeneous sphere of action. And thus must I actually regard the will in the present sensuous world, the only world known to me. I am indeed compelled to believe, and consequently to act as if I thought, that by my mere volition my tongue, my hand, or my foot may be set in motion; but how a mere aspiration, an impress of intelligence upon itself, such as will is, can be the principle of motion to a heavy material mass—this I not only find impossible to conceive, but the mere assertion is, before the tribunal of the understanding, a palpable absurdity. Here the movement of matter, even in myself, can be explained only by the internal forces of matter itself.

Such a view of my will as I have taken, however, is not attained merely through the conviction that the will is the highest active principle for this world—which it certainly might be, without having freedom in itself, by the mere energy of the system of the universe, such as we must conceive of the formative power in Nature. The will rejects absolutely all earthly purposes, all purposes lying outside itself, and recognizes itself, for its own sake, as its own ultimate end. By such a view of my will I am at once directed to a supersensual order of things in which the will, by itself alone and without any instrument lying outside of itself, becomes an efficient cause in a sphere which, like itself, is purely spiritual, and is thoroughly accessible to it. That moral volition is demanded of us absolutely for its own sake alone—a truth which I discover only as a fact in my inward consciousness, and to the knowledge of which I cannot attain in any other way: this was the first step of my thought. That this demand is reasonable, and the source and standard of all else that is reasonable; that it is not modeled upon any other thing whatever, but that all other things must, on the contrary, model themselves upon it, and be dependent upon it—a conviction which, again, I cannot arrive at from without, but can attain only by inward experience, by means of the unhesitating and immovable assent which I freely accord to this demand—this was the second step of my thought. And from these two terms I have attained to faith in a supersensual Eternal World. If I abandon the former, the latter falls to the ground. If it were true—as many say it is, assuming it without further proof as self-evident and extolling it as the highest summit of human wisdom—that all human virtue must have before it a certain definite external object, and that it must first be assured of the possibility of attaining this object, before it can act and before it can become virtue; and if, consequently, reason by no means contained within itself the principle and the standard of its own activity, but were forced to receive this standard from without through contemplation of an external world—if this were true, then the ultimate end of our existence might be accomplished here below: human nature might be completely developed and exhausted by our earthly vocation, and we should have no rational ground for raising our thoughts above the present life.

What I have said to myself just now could also be said by some thinker who, moved perhaps by mere love for the new and unusual, acquired these first principles historically from some place or other and was able to deduce their consequences. But he would present us with the thoughts of some other being, not with his own; everything would float before him empty and without significance, because he would be without the sense whereby he might apprehend its reality. It is as if he were a blind man, who, upon certain true principles concerning colors which he has learned historically, has built a perfectly correct theory of color, even though no color exists for him in reality; he can tell how, under certain conditions, it *must be;* but to him it *is* not so, because he does not stand under these conditions. The faculty by which we lay hold on Eternal Life is to be attained only by actually renouncing the sensuous and its objects, and sacrificing them to that law which takes cognizance of our will only and not of our actions; renouncing them with the firmest conviction that it is reasonable for us to do so—nay, that it is the only thing reasonable for us. By this renunciation of what is earthly, faith in the Eternal first arises in our soul, and is there enshrined apart, as the only support to which we can cling after we have given up all else, as the only animating principle that can elevate our minds and inspire our lives. We must indeed, according to the figure of a sacred doctrine, first "die unto the world and be born again, before we can enter the kingdom of God."

I see—I now see clearly before me the cause of my former indifference and blindness concerning spiritual things. Absorbed by mere earthly objects, lost in them with all our thoughts and efforts, moved and urged onward only by the notion of a result lying beyond ourselves, by the desire of such a result and of our own enjoyment therein, insensible and dead to the pure impulse of reason which gives a law to itself and offers to our aspirations a purely spiritual end, the immortal Psyche remains with fettered pinions fastened to the earth. Our philosophy becomes the history of our own heart and life; and according to what we ourselves are do we conceive of man and his vocation. Never impelled by any motive other than the desire after what can be

actually realized in this world, there is for us no true freedom—no freedom which holds the ground of its determination absolutely and entirely within itself. Our
freedom is, at best, that of the self-forming plant; not
essentially higher in its nature, but only more elabo-
rate in its results; producing not a mere material form
with roots, leaves, and blossoms, but a mind with impulses,
thoughts, and actions. We cannot have the slightest conception of true freedom, because we do not ourselves possess it; when it is spoken of, we either bring down what is
said to the level of our own notions, or at once declare all
such talk to be nonsense. Without the idea of freedom, we
are likewise without the faculty for another world. Everything of this kind floats past before us like words that are
not addressed to us; like a pale shadow, without color or
meaning, which we know not how to lay hold of or retain.
We leave it as we find it, without the least participation
or sympathy. Or should we ever be urged by a more active
zeal to consider it seriously, we then convince ourselves to
our own satisfaction that all such ideas are untenable and
worthless reveries which the man of sound understanding
unhesitatingly rejects; and according to the premises from
which we proceed, made up as they are of our inward ex-
periences, we are perfectly in the right and secure from
either refutation or conversion so long as we remain what
we are. The excellent doctrines which are taught among
us with a special authority, concerning freedom, duty, and
everlasting life, become to us romantic fables, like those
of Tartarus and the Elysian fields; although we do not pub-
lish to the world this our secret opinion, because we find
it expedient, by means of these figures, to maintain an outward decorum among the populace; or, should we be less
reflective, and ourselves bound in the chains of authority,
then we sink to the level of the common mind, and believ-
ing what, *thus understood*, would be mere foolish fables,

we find in those pure spiritual symbols only the promise of continuing throughout eternity the same miserable existence which we possess here below.

In one word: only by the fundamental improvement of my will does a new light arise within me concerning my existence and vocation; without this, however much I may speculate, and with whatever rare intellectual gifts I may be endowed, darkness remains within me and around me. The improvement of the heart alone leads to true wisdom. Let then my whole life be unceasingly devoted to this one purpose.

IV

My lawful will, merely as such, in and through itself, shall certainly and invariably produce consequences; every determination of my will in accordance with duty, although no action should follow it, shall operate in another, to me incomprehensible, world in which nothing but this moral determination of the will shall possess efficient activity. What is it that is assumed in this conception?

Obviously a *law*—a rule absolutely without exception, according to which a will determined by duty must have consequences; just as in the material world which surrounds me I assume a law according to which this ball when thrown by my hand with this particular force, in this particular direction, necessarily moves in such a direction with a certain degree of velocity—perhaps strikes another ball with a certain amount of force, which in its turn moves on with a certain velocity, and so on. As here, in the mere direction and motion of my hand, I already recognize and apprehend all the consequent directions and movements with the same certainty as if they were already present before me, even so do I embrace by means of my virtuous will a series of necessary and inevitable consequences in the spiritual world as if they were already present before me; but I cannot define them as I do those in the material world. I know only that they must be, but not *how* they shall be; and even in knowing this I conceive of a *law* of the spiritual world in which my pure will is one of the moving forces, as my hand is one of the moving forces of the material world. My own firm confidence in these results and the conceptions of this *law* of a spiritual world are one and the same; they are not two thoughts, one of which arises by means of the other, but they are entirely the same thought, just as the confidence with which I calculate on a certain motion in a material body and the conception of a mechanical law of nature on which that motion depends are one and the same. The conception of a *law* expresses nothing more than the firm, immovable confidence of reason in a principle, and the absolute impossibility of admitting its opposite.

I assume such a law of a spiritual world—not given by my will nor by the will of any finite being, nor by the will of all finite beings taken together, but a law to which my will, and the will of all finite beings, is subject. Neither I, nor any finite and therefore sensuous being, can conceive how a mere will can have consequences, nor what may be the true nature of those consequences; for herein consists the essential character of our finite nature—that we are unable to conceive this, that, having indeed our will as such wholly within our power, we are yet compelled by our sensuous nature to regard the consequences of that will as sensuous states. How, then, can I or any finite being whatever propose as object, and thereby give reality to, something we can neither imagine nor conceive? I cannot say that, in the material world, my hand, or any other body which belongs to that world and is subject to the universal law of gravity, brings this law into operation; these bodies themselves stand under this law and are able to set another body in motion only in accordance with this law, and only in so far as that body, by virtue of this law, partakes of the universal moving power of Nature. Just as little can a finite will give a law to the supersensual world which no finite spirit can embrace; but all finite wills stand under the law of that world and can produce results therein only inasmuch as that law already exists, and inasmuch as they themselves, in accordance with the form of that law which is applicable to finite wills, bring themselves under its conditions and within the sphere of its activity by moral obedience—by moral obedience, I say, the only tie which unites them to that higher world, the only nerve that descends from it to them, and the only organ through which they can react upon it. As the universal power of attraction embraces all bodies and holds them together in themselves and with each other, and the movement of each separate body is possible only on the supposition of this power, so does that supersensual law unite, hold together, and embrace all finite reasonable beings. My will, and the will of all finite beings, may be regarded from a double point of view: partly as a mere *volition*, an internal act directed upon itself alone, and in so far the will is complete in itself, concluded in this act of volition; and partly as something beyond this, a *fact*. It assumes the latter form to me as soon as I regard it as completed, but it must also become so beyond me; in the *world of sense*, as the moving principle, for instance, of my hand, from the movement of which again other movements follow; in the *supersensual world*, as the principle of a series of spiritual consequences of which I have no conception. In the former point of view, as a mere act of volition, it stands wholly within my own power; its assumption of the latter character, that of an active first principle, depends not upon me, but on a law to which I myself am subject— on the law of nature in the world of sense, on a supersensual law in the world of pure thought.

What, then, is this law of the spiritual world which I conceive? This idea now stands before me in fixed and perfect shape; I cannot and dare not add anything whatever to it; I have only to express and interpret it distinctly. It is obviously not such as I may suppose the principle of my own, or any other possible sensuous world, to be—a fixed, inert existence, altogether different from a mere will, something from which by the encounter of a will an internal power may be evolved. For—and this is the substance of my belief—my will, absolutely by itself, and without the intervention of any instrument that might weaken its expression, shall act in a perfectly congenial sphere; reason shall act upon reason, spirit upon spirit, in a sphere to which nevertheless my will does not give the law of life, activity, and progress, but which has that law in itself; my will shall act, therefore, upon self-active reason. But self-active reason is will. The law of the supersensual world must, therefore, be a *will*—a will which operates purely as will, by itself and absolutely, without any instrument or sensible material of its activity; which is at the same time both act and product; with whom to "will" is to do, to command is to execute; in which, therefore, the instinctive demand of reason for absolute freedom and independence is realized; a will which in itself is law, determined by no fancy or caprice, through no previous reflection, hesitation, or doubt, but eternal, unchangeable, on which we may securely and infallibly rely as the physical man relies with certainty on the laws of his world; a will in which the moral will of finite beings, and this alone, has sure and unfailing results; since for all else it is unavailing and for it all else is as nothing.

That sublime will thus pursues no solitary path withdrawn from the other parts of the world of reason. There is a spiritual bond between Him and all finite rational beings; and He himself is this spiritual bond of the rational universe. Let me will, purely and decidedly, my duty; and He wills that, in the spiritual world at least, my will shall prosper. Every moral resolution of a finite being goes up before Him, and—to speak after the manner of mortals—

moves and determines Him, not in consequence of a momentary satisfaction, but in accordance with the eternal law of His being. With surprising clearness does this thought, which hitherto was veiled in obscurity, now reveal itself to my soul—the thought that my will, merely as such and through itself, shall have results. It has results because it is immediately and infallibly perceived by another will to which it is related, which is its own accomplishment and the only living principle of the spiritual world; *in Him* it has its first results, and *through Him* it acquires an influence on the whole spiritual world, which throughout is but a product of that Infinite Will.

Thus do I approach—the mortal must speak in his own language—thus do I approach that Infinite Will; and the voice of conscience in my soul, which teaches me in every situation of life what I have there to do, is the channel through which again His influence descends upon me. That voice, made audible by my environment and translated into my language, is the oracle of the Eternal World which announces to me how I am to perform my part in the order of the spiritual universe, or in the Infinite Will who is Himself that order. I cannot, indeed, survey or comprehend that spiritual order, and I need not do so; I am but a link in its chain and can no more judge of the whole than a single tone of music can judge of the entire harmony of which it forms a part. But what I myself ought to be in this harmony of spirits I must know, for it is only I myself who can make me so—and this is immediately revealed to me by a voice whose tones descend upon me from that other world. Thus do I stand connected with the One who alone has existence, and thus do I participate in His being. There is nothing real, lasting, imperishable in me, save these two elements: the voice of conscience, and my free obedience. By the first, the spiritual world bows down to me and embraces me as one of its members; by the second, I raise myself into this world, apprehend it, and react upon it. That

Infinite Will is the mediator between it and me; for He Himself is the original source of both it and me. This is the one True and Imperishable for which my soul yearns even from its inmost depths; all else is mere appearance, ever vanishing, and ever returning in a new semblance.

This Will binds me in union with Himself; He also binds me in union with all finite beings like myself, and is the common mediator between us all. This is the great mystery of the invisible world, and its fundamental law, in so far as it is a world or system of many individual wills: *the union and direct reciprocal action of many separate and independent wills*—a mystery which already lies clearly before every eye in the present life, without attracting the notice of anyone, or being regarded as in any way wonderful. The voice of conscience, which imposes on each his particular duty, is the beam of light on which we come forth from the bosom of the Infinite and assume our place as particular individual beings; it fixes the limits of our personality; it is thus the true original element of our nature, the foundation and material of all our life. The absolute freedom of the will, which we bring down with us from the Infinite into the world of Time, is the principle of this our life. I act. The sensible intuition through which alone I become a personal intelligence being supposed, it is easy to conceive how I must necessarily know of this my action; I know it because it is I myself who act; it is easy to conceive how, by means of this sensible intuition, my spiritual *act* appears to me as a *fact in the world of sense,* and how, on the other hand, by the same intuition, the law of duty, which in itself is a purely spiritual law, should appear to me as *the command to such an act;* it is easy to conceive how an actually present world should appear to me as the condition of this act and, in part, as the consequence and product of it. Thus far I remain within myself and upon my own territory; everything here which has an existence for me unfolds itself purely and solely from myself; I see everywhere only myself, and no true existence external to me. But in this my world I admit also the operations of other beings, as separate and independent of me as I am of them. How these beings can themselves know of the influences which proceed from them may easily be conceived; they know of them in the same way in which I know of my own. But how I can know of *them* is absolutely inconceivable; just as it is inconceivable how *they* can possess that knowledge of *my* existence and its manifestations, which nevertheless I ascribe to them. How do they come within my world, or I within theirs? The principle by which the consciousness of ourselves, of our operations, and of their sensuous conditions is deduced from ourselves —i.e., the principle that each individual must undoubtedly know what he himself does—is here wholly inapplicable. How have free spirits knowledge of free spirits? We know that free spirits are the only reality, and that an independent world of sense, through which they might act on each other, is no longer to be taken into account. Or shall it be said, I perceive reasonable beings like myself by the changes which they produce in the world of sense? Then I ask again: How do you perceive these changes? I comprehend very well how you can perceive changes which are brought about by the mere mechanism of nature; for the law of this mechanism is no other than the law of your own thought, according to which, this world being once assumed, it is carried out into further developments. But the changes of which we now speak are not brought about by the mere mechanism of nature, but by a free will elevated above nature; and only in so far as you can regard them in this character can you infer from them the existence of free beings like yourself. Where then is the law within yourself, according to which you can realize the determinations of other wills absolutely independent of you? In short, this mutual recognition and reciprocal action of free beings in this world is perfectly inexplicable by the laws of nature or of thought, and can be explained only through the One in whom they are united while separate from each other; through the Infinite Will who sustains and embraces them all in His own sphere. The knowledge we have of each other does not flow immediately from you to me, or from me to you; we are separated by an insurmountable barrier. Only through the common fountain of our spiritual being do we know of each other; only in Him do we recognize each other and influence each other. "Respect here the image of freedom upon the earth—here a work which bears its impress." Thus it is proclaimed within me by the voice of that Will which speaks to me only in so far as it imposes duties upon me. The only principle through which I recognize you and your work is the command of conscience to respect you.

Whence, then, our feelings, our sensible intuitions, our discursive laws of thought—upon which is founded the external world we behold and in which we believe that we exert an influence on each other? With respect to the last two—our sensible intuitions and our laws of thought—to say these are laws of reason in itself is to give no satisfactory answer at all. For us, indeed, who are excluded from the pure domain of reason in itself, it may be impossible to think otherwise or to conceive of reason under any other law. But the true law of reason in itself is the practical law, the law of the supersensual world, or of that sublime Will. And, leaving this for a moment undecided, whence comes our universal agreement as to feelings, which, nevertheless, are something positive, immediate, inexplicable? That we all behold the same world of sense—this depends upon our agreement: in feeling, in perception, and in the laws of thought.

"It is a harmonious, although inconceivable, limitation of the finite rational beings who compose our species; and only by means of such a harmonious limitation do they become a species"—thus answers the philosophy of mere knowledge, and here it must rest as its highest point. But what can set a limit to reason but reason itself? What can limit all finite reason but the Infinite Reason? This universal agreement concerning a sensible world, assumed and accepted by us as the foundation of all our other life and as the sphere of our duty, is, strictly considered, just as incomprehensible as our unanimity concerning the products of our reciprocal freedom; this agreement is the result of the One Eternal Infinite Will. Our faith, of which we have spoken as faith in duty, is only faith in Him, in His reason, in His truth. What, then, is the peculiar and essential truth which we accept in the world of sense, and in which we believe? Nothing less than that from our free and faithful performance of our duty in this world there will arise to us throughout eternity a life in which our freedom and morality may still continue their development. If this be true, then indeed is there truth in our world, and the only truth possible for finite beings; and it must be true, for this world is the result of the Eternal Will in us—and that Will, by the law of His own being, can have no other purpose with respect to finite beings than that which we have set forth.

That Eternal Will is thus assuredly the Creator of the World, in the only way in which He can be so, and in the only way in which it needs creation: in the finite reason. Those who regard Him as building up a world from an everlasting inert matter, which must still remain inert and lifeless, like a vessel made by human hands, not an eternal procession of His self-development, or who ascribe to Him the production of a material universe out of nothing, know neither the world nor Him. If matter can be the only reality, then indeed there is nothing, and throughout all eternity there can be nothing. Reason alone exists: the Infinite in Himself, the finite in Him and through Him.

Only in our minds has He created a world; at least that *from which* we unfold it—and that *by which* we unfold it— the voice of duty, and harmonious feelings, intuitions, and laws of thought. It is His light through which we behold the light and all that it reveals to us. In our minds He still creates this world, and acts upon it by acting upon our minds through the call of duty as soon as another free being changes anything whatsoever therein. In our minds He upholds this world, and thereby the finite existence of which alone we are capable, by continually evolving from each state of our existence other states in succession. When He shall have sufficiently proved us, according to His supreme designs, for our next succeeding vocation, and we shall have sufficiently cultivated ourselves for entering upon it, then, by that which we call death, will He annihilate for us this life and introduce us to a new life, the product of our virtuous actions. All our life is His life. We are in His hand and abide therein, and no one can pluck us out of His hand. We are eternal, because He is eternal.

Sublime and Living Will! named by no name, compassed by no thought! I may well raise my soul to Thee, for Thou and I are not divided. Thy voice sounds within me, mine resounds in Thee; and all my thoughts, if they be but good and true, live in Thee also. In Thee, the Incomprehensible, I myself and the world in which I live become clearly comprehensible to me; all the secrets of my existence are laid open, and perfect harmony arises in my soul.

Thou art best known to the childlike, devoted, simple mind. To it Thou art the searcher of hearts, who seest its inmost depths; the ever-present true witness of its thoughts, who knowest its truth, who knowest it though all the world know it not. Thou art the Father who ever desirest its good, who rulest all things for the best. To Thy will it unhesitatingly resigns itself: "Do with me," it says, "what Thou wilt; I know that it is good, for it is Thou who doest it." The inquisitive understanding, which has heard of Thee, but seen Thee not, would teach us Thy nature, and as Thy image shows us a monstrous and incongruous shape, which the sagacious laugh at and the wise and good abhor.

I hide my face before Thee, and lay my hand upon my mouth. *How* Thou art, and seemest to Thine own being, I can never know, any more than I can assume Thy nature. After thousands upon thousands of spirit-lives, I shall comprehend Thee as little as I do now in this earthly house. That which I conceive becomes finite through my very conception of it; and this can never, even by endless exaltation, rise into the Infinite. Thou differest from men, not in degree but in nature. In every stage of their advancement they think of Thee as a greater *man,* and still a greater; but never as God—the Infinite whom no measure can mete. I have only this discursive, progressive thought, and I can conceive of no other. How can I venture to ascribe it to Thee? In the Idea of *person* there are imperfections, limitations—how can I clothe Thee with it without these?

I will not attempt that which the imperfection of my finite nature forbids, and which would be useless to me: *How* Thou art, I may not know. But let me be what I ought to be, and Thy relations to me—the mortal—and to all mortals, lie open before my eyes and surround me more clearly than the consciousness of my own existence. *Thou workest* in me the knowledge of my duty, of my vocation in the world of reasonable beings; *how,* I know not, nor need I to know. *Thou knowest* what I think and what I will: *how* Thou canst know, through what act thou bringest about that consciousness, I cannot understand—nay, I know that the idea of an act, of a particular act of consciousness belongs to me alone, and not to Thee, the Infinite One. *Thou willest* that my free obedience shall bring with it eternal consequences: the act of Thy will I cannot comprehend, I know only that it is not like mine. *Thou doest,* and Thy will itself is the deed; but the way of Thy working is not as my ways—I cannot trace it. *Thou livest and art,* for Thou knowest and willest and workest, omnipresent to finite Reason; but Thou *art not* as I now and always must conceive of being.

In the contemplation of these Thy relations to me, the finite being, will I rest in calm blessedness. I know immediately only what I ought to do. This will I do, freely, joyfully, and without cavilling or sophistry, for it is Thy voice which commands me to do it; it is the part assigned to me in the spiritual Worldplan; and the power with which I shall perform it is Thy power. Whatever may be commanded by that voice, whatever executed by that power, is, in that plan, assuredly and truly good. I remain tranquil amid all the events of this world, for they are in Thy world. Nothing can perplex or surprise or dishearten me, as surely as Thou livest, and I can behold Thy life. For in Thee, and through Thee, O Infinite One, I see even my present world in another light. Nature and natural consequences in the destinies and conduct of free beings—these words become unmeaning in relation to you. Nature is no longer; Thou, only Thou, art. It no longer appears to me to be the end and purpose of the present world to bring about that state of universal peace among men, and of unlimited dominion over the mechanism of Nature, for its own sake alone; it is, rather, that this should be brought about by men themselves; and, since the duty is laid upon *all,* that it should be brought about by *all,* as one great, free, moral community. Nothing new and better for an individual shall be attainable except through his own virtuous will; nothing new and better for a community except through the common will being in accordance with duty—this is a fundamental law of the great moral empire of which the present life is a part. The good will of the individual is thus often lost to this world because it is only the will of the individual, and the will of the majority is not in har-

mony with his—and then its results are to be found solely
in a future world; while even the passions and vices of men
co-operate in the attainment of good—not in and for themselves, for in this sense good can never come out of evil,
but by holding the balance against the opposite vices, and,
at last, by their excess, annihilating these antagonists and
themselves with them. Oppression could never have gained
the upper hand in human affairs unless the cowardice, base-
ness, and mutual mistrust of men had smoothed the way
to it. It will continue to increase until it extirpate cowardice and slavishness, and despair itself at last reawaken
courage. Then shall the two opposite vices have annihilated
each other, and the noblest of all human relations, lasting
freedom, come forth from their antagonism.

The actions of free beings, strictly considered, have results only in other free beings; for in them, and for them
alone, there is a world; and that in which they all accord
is itself the world. But they have these results only through
the Infinite Will—the medium through which all individual
beings influence each other. But the announcement, the
revelation of this Will to us, is always a call to a particular
duty. Thus even what we call evil in the world, the consequence of the abuse of freedom, exists only through this
Will; and it exists for those who experience it only in so
far as, through it, duties are laid upon them. Were it not
in the eternal plan of our moral culture, and of the culture
of our whole race, that precisely these duties should be
laid upon us, they would not be so laid upon us; and that
through which they are laid upon us—i.e., what we call evil
—would not even have arisen. In so far, everything that *is*
is good and absolutely legitimate. There is but one world
possible—a thoroughly good world. All that happens in this
world is subservient to the improvement and culture of
man and, by means of this, to the promotion of the purpose of his earthly existence. It is this higher Worldplan
which we call Nature when we say: Nature leads men

through want to industry; through the evils of general disorder to a just constitution; through the miseries of continual wars to endless peace on earth. Thy will, Infinite One, thy Providence alone, is this higher Nature. This, too, is best understood by artless simplicity, when it regards this life as a place of trial and culture, as a school for eternity; when, in all the events of life, the most trivial as well as the most important, it beholds Thy guiding Providence disposing all for the best; when it firmly believes that all things must work together for the good of those who love their duty, and who know Thee.

Oh! I have, indeed, dwelt in darkness during the past days of my life. I have, indeed, heaped error upon error and imagined myself wise. Now, for the first time, I wholly understand the doctrine which from thy lips, wonderful Spirit, seemed so strange to me, although my understanding had nothing to oppose to it; for now, for the first time, I comprehend it in its whole compass, in its deepest foundations, and through all its consequences.

Man is not a product of the world of sense, and the end of his existence cannot be attained in it. His vocation transcends time and space, and everything that pertains to sense. What he is, and to what he is to train himself, of that he must know; as his vocation is a lofty one, he must be able to raise his thoughts above the limitations of sense. He must accomplish it: where his being finds its home, there his thoughts, too, seek their dwelling place; and the truly human mode of thought, that which alone is worthy of him, that in which his whole spiritual strength is manifested, is that whereby he raises himself above those limitations, whereby all that pertains to sense vanishes into nothing—into a mere reflection in mortal eyes of the one, abiding Infinite.

Many have raised themselves to this mode of thought,

without scientific inquiry, merely by their nobleness of heart and their pure moral instinct, because their lives have been pre-eminently lives of feeling and sentiment. By their conduct, they have denied the efficiency and reality of the world of sense and made it of no account in regulating their resolutions and their actions, even though they have not made it clear, by reasoning, that this world has no existence for the intellect. Those who could dare to say, "Our citizenship is in heaven; we have here no continuing city, but we seek one to come"; those whose chief principle it was "to die to the world, to be born again, and already here below to enter upon a new life"—certainly set no value whatever on the things of sense and were, to use the language of the Schools, practical Transcendental Idealists.

Others who, besides possessing the natural proneness to mere sensuous activity, which is common to us all, have strengthened it by their habits of thought, until they have grown with it and become entangled in it, can raise themselves above it, permanently and completely, only by persistent and conclusive thought; otherwise, with the purest moral intentions, they would be continually drawn down again by their understanding, and their whole being would remain a prolonged and insoluble contradiction. For these the philosophy which I now, for the first time, thoroughly understand will be the power that shall first set free the imprisoned Psyche and unfold her wings, so that, hovering for a moment above her former self, she may cast a glance on her abandoned slough, and then soar upwards thenceforward to live and move in higher spheres.

Blessed be the hour in which I first resolved to inquire into myself and my vocation. All my doubts are solved; I know what I can know, and have no apprehensions regarding that which I cannot know. I am satisfied; perfect harmony and clearness reign in my soul, and a new and more glorious spiritual existence begins for me.

My complete vocation I cannot comprehend; what I shall be hereafter transcends all my thoughts. A part of that vocation is concealed from me; it is visible only to One, to the Father of Spirits, to whose care it is committed. I know only that it is sure, and that it is eternal and glorious like Himself. But that part of it which is confided to myself I know, and know it thoroughly, for it is the root of all my other knowledge. I know assuredly, in every moment of my life, what I ought to do; and this is my whole vocation, in so far as it depends on me. From this point, since my knowledge does not reach beyond it, I shall not depart; I shall desire to know nothing beyond this; I shall take my stand upon this central point and firmly root myself here. To this shall all my thoughts and endeavors, my whole powers, be directed; my whole existence shall be interwoven with it.

I ought, as far as in me lies, to cultivate my understanding and to acquire knowledge, but only with the purpose of preparing thereby within me a larger field and wider sphere of duty. I ought to desire to have much, in order that much may be required of me. I ought to exercise my powers and capacities in every possible way, but only in order to render myself a more serviceable and fitting instrument of duty; for until the commandment shall have been realized in the outward world by means of my whole personality, I am answerable for it to my conscience. I ought to exhibit in myself, as far as I am able, humanity in all its completeness, not for the mere sake of humanity, which in itself has not the slightest worth, but in order that virtue, which alone has worth in itself, may be exhibited in its highest perfection in human nature. I ought to regard myself, body and soul, with all that is in me or that belongs to me, only as a means of duty; and desire only to perform that duty and to make myself able to perform it, as far as in me lies. But when the commandment—provided only that it shall have been in truth the commandment which I have obeyed, and I have been really conscious only of the pure, single intention of obeying it—when the commandment shall have been passed beyond my personal being to its realization in the outside world, then I have no more anxiety about it, for thenceforward it is committed into the hands of the Eternal Will. Further care or anxiety would be but idle self-torment, would be unbelief and distrust of that Infinite Will. I shall never dream of governing the world in His stead, of listening to the voice of my own imperfect wisdom instead of to His voice in my conscience, or of substituting the partial views of a shortsighted creature for His vast plan which embraces the universe. I know that thereby I should lose my own place in His order, and in the order of all spiritual being.

As with calmness and devotion I reverence this higher Providence, so in my actions I ought to reverence the freedom of other beings around me. The question for me is not what they, according to my conceptions, ought to do; but what I may venture to do in order to induce them to do it. I can desire only to act on their conviction and their will as far as the order of society and their own consent will permit, but I can by no means desire to influence their powers and relations without their conviction and consent. They do what they do on their own responsibility; with this I neither can nor dare interfere, and the Eternal Will will dispose all for the best. It concerns me more to respect their freedom than to hinder or prevent what to me seems evil in its use.

In this point of view I become a new creature, and my whole relations to the existing world are changed. The ties by which my mind was formerly united to this world, and by whose secret guidance I followed all its movements, are forever sundered, and I stand free, calm, and immovable, a universe to myself. I apprehend outward objects and am connected with them, no longer by my heart but by my eye alone; and this eye itself is purified by freedom, and looks through error and deformity to the true and beautiful, as upon the unruffled surface of water shapes are more purely mirrored in a milder light.

My mind is forever closed to confusion and perplexity, to uncertainty, doubt, and anxiety; my heart is closed to grief, repentance, and desire. There is but one thing that I may know—namely, what I ought to do; and this I always know infallibly. Concerning all else I know nothing, and know that I know nothing. I firmly root myself in this my ignorance and refrain from harassing myself with conjectures concerning that of which I know nothing. No occurrence in this world can affect me either with joy or sorrow; calm and unmoved, I look down upon all things, for I know that I cannot explain a single event, nor comprehend its connection with that which alone concerns me. All that happens belongs to the plan of the Eternal World, and is good in its place; that much I know. What in this plan is pure gain, what is only a means for the removal of some existing evil, what therefore ought to afford me more or less satisfaction, I know not. In His world all things prosper; this satisfies me, and in this belief I stand fast as a rock. But what in His world is merely the germ, what the blossom and what the fruit itself, I know not.

The only matter in which I can be concerned is the progress of reason and morality in the world of reasonable beings; and this only for its own sake, for the sake of this progress. Whether I or someone else be the instrument of this progress, whether it be my deed or that of another by which it is promoted or hindered, is of no importance to me. I regard myself merely as one of the instruments for carrying out the purpose of reason; I respect, love, or feel an interest in myself only as such an instrument, and desire the successful issue of my deed only in so far as it promotes this purpose. In like manner, I regard all the events of this world only with reference to this one purpose, whether they proceed from me or from others, whether they relate directly to me or to others. My breast is steeled against annoyance on account of personal offenses and vexations, or exultation in personal merit; for my whole personality has disappeared in the contemplation of the purpose of my being.

Should it ever seem to me as if truth had been put to silence and virtue expelled from the world, as if folly and vice had now summoned all their powers and even assumed the place of reason and true wisdom; should it happen that just when all good men looked with hope for the regeneration of the human race, everything should become even worse than it had been before; should the work, well and happily begun, on which the eyes of all true-minded men were fixed with joyous expectation, suddenly and unexpectedly be changed into the vilest forms of evil—these things will not disturb me. And as little will I be persuaded to indulge in idleness, neglect, or false security on account of an apparently rapid growth of enlightenment, a seeming diffusion of freedom and independence, an increase of more gentle manners, peacefulness, docility and general moderation among men, as if now everything were attained. Thus it appears to me; or rather it is so—it is actually so to me; and I know in both cases, as indeed I know in all possible cases, what I have next to do. As to everything else, I rest in the most perfect tranquility, for I know nothing whatever about any other thing. Those, to me, so sorrowful events may, in the plan of the Eternal One, be the direct means for the attainment of a good result—that strife of evil against good may be their last decisive struggle, and it may be permitted to the former to assemble all its powers for this encounter only to lose them, and thereby to exhibit itself in all its impotence. These, to me, joyful appearances may rest on very uncertain foundations; what I had taken for enlightenment may perhaps be but hollow superficiality and aversion to all true ideas; what I had taken for independence, but unbridled passion; what I had taken for gentleness and moderation, but weakness and indolence. I do not indeed know this, but it might be so; and then I should have as little cause to mourn over the one as to rejoice over the other. But I do know that I live in a world which belongs to the Supreme Wisdom and Goodness, who thoroughly comprehends its plan and will infallibly accomplish it; and in this conviction I rest, and am blessed.

That there are free beings, destined to reason and morality, who strive against reason and call forth all their powers to the support of folly and vice, just as little will this disturb me and stir up within me indignation and wrath. The perversity which would hate what is good because it is good, and promote evil merely from a love of evil as such —this perversity which alone could excite my just anger, I ascribe to no one who bears the form of man, for I know that it does not lie in human nature. I know that for all who act thus there is really, in so far as they act thus, neither good nor evil, but only an agreeable or disagreeable feeling; that they do not stand under their own dominion, but under the power of Nature; and that it is not themselves but this Nature in them which with all its strength seeks the pleasure and flies from the pain, without regard to whether it be otherwise good or evil. I know that, being once for all what they are, they cannot act in any respect otherwise than as they do act, and I am very far from getting angry with necessity, or indulging in wrath against blind and unconscious Nature. Herein truly lies their guilt and unworthiness, that they are what they are; and that, in place of being free and independent, they have resigned themselves to the current of mere natural impulse.

It is this alone which could excite my indignation, but

here I should fall into absolute absurdity. I cannot call them to account for their want of freedom without first attributing to them the power of making themselves free. I wish to be angry with them, and find no object for my wrath. What they actually are does not deserve my anger; what might deserve it they are not, and they would not deserve it if they were. My displeasure would strike an impalpable nonentity. I must indeed always treat them, and address them, as if they were what I well know they are not; I must always suppose in them that whereby alone I can approach them and communicate with them. Duty commands me to act toward them according to a conception of them which is contrary to that I achieve when I contemplate them. And thus it may certainly happen that I turn toward them with a noble indignation, as if they were free, in order to arouse within them a similar indignation against themselves—an indignation which in my own heart I cannot reasonably entertain. It is only the acting, social man within me whose anger is excited by folly and vice; not the contemplative man who reposes undisturbed in the calm serenity of his own spirit.

Should I be visited by corporeal suffering, pain, or disease, I cannot avoid *feeling* them, for they are accidents of my nature; and as long as I remain here below I am a part of Nature. But they shall not *grieve* me. They can touch only the Nature with which in a wonderful manner I am united —not myself, the being exalted above all Nature. The sure end of all pain, and of all sensibility to pain, is death; and of all things which the mere natural man is wont to regard as evils, this is to me the least. I shall not die for myself, but only for others—for those who remain behind, from whose fellowship I am torn. For myself the hour of Death is the hour of Birth to a new, more excellent life.

Now that my heart is closed against all desire for earthly things, now that I have no longer any sense for the transitory and perishable, the universe appears before my eyes clothed in a more glorious form. The dead inert mass, which only filled up space, has vanished: and in its place there flows onward, with the rushing music of mighty waves, an endless stream of life and power and action, which issues from the original Source of all life—from Thy Life, Infinite One, for all life is Thy Life, and only the religious eye penetrates to the realm of true Beauty.

I am related to Thee, and all that I behold around me is related to me; all is life and soul, and regards me with clear spirit-eyes, and speaks with spirit-voices to my heart. In all the forms that surround me, I behold the reflection of my own being broken up into countless diversified shapes, as the morning sun, broken in a thousand dew-drops, throws back its splendors to itself.

Thy Life, as alone the finite mind can conceive it, is self-forming, self-manifesting Will; this Life, clothed to the eye of the mortal with manifold sensible forms, flows through me and throughout the immeasurable universe of Nature. Here it streams as self-creating and self-forming matter through my veins and muscles and pours out its abundance into the tree, the plant, the grass. Creative life flows forth in one continuous stream, drop on drop, through all forms and into all places where my eye can follow it; it reveals itself to me, in a different shape in each various corner of the universe, as the same power by which in secret darkness my own frame was formed. There, in free play, it leaps and dances as spontaneous activity in the animal and manifests itself in each new form as a new, peculiar, self-subsisting world: the same power which, invisibly to me, moves and animates my own frame. Everything that lives and moves follows this universal impulse, this one principle of all motion, which guides the harmonious convulsion from one end of the universe to the other. In the animal, this takes place *without freedom;* in me, from whom in the visible world motion proceeds without having its source in me, it takes place *with freedom.*

But pure and holy, and as near to Thine own nature as anything can be to mortal eye, does this Thy Life flow forth as the bond which unites spirit with spirit, as the breath and atmosphere of a rational world, unimaginable and incomprehensible, and yet there, clearly visible to the spiritual eye. Borne onward in this stream of light, thought floats from soul to soul without pause or variation, and returns purer and brighter from each kindred mind. Through this mysterious union does each individual perceive, understand, and love himself only in another; each soul unfolds itself only through its fellows, and there are no longer individual men, but only one humanity; no individual thought or love or hate, but only thought, love and hate, in and through each other. Through this wondrous influence the affinity of spirits in the invisible world permeates even their physical nature; manifests itself in two sexes, which, even if that spiritual bond could be torn asunder, would, simply as creatures of nature, be compelled to love each other; flows forth in the tenderness of parents and children, brothers and sisters, as if the souls were of one blood like the bodies, and their minds were branches and blossoms of the same stem; and from these it embraces, in narrower or wider circles, the whole sentient world. Even at the root of their hate, there lies a secret thirst after love; and no enmity springs up but from friendship denied.

Through that which to others seems a mere dead mass, my eye beholds this eternal life and movement in every vein of sensible and spiritual Nature, and sees this life rising in ever-increasing growth, and ever purifying itself to a more spiritual expression. The universe is to me no longer what it was before—the ever-recurring circle, the eternally-repeated play, the monster swallowing itself up only to bring itself forth again; it has become transfigured before me, and now bears the one stamp of spiritual life—a constant progress toward higher perfection in a line that runs out into the Infinite.

The sun rises and sets, the stars sink and reappear, the spheres hold their circle-dance; but they do not return as they were when they disappeared, and even in the bright fountain of life itself there is life and progress. Every hour which they lead on, every morning and every evening, sinks with new increase upon the world; new life and new love descend from the spheres like dewdrops from the clouds, and encircle nature as the cool night the earth.

All death in Nature is birth, and in death itself appears visibly the exaltation of life. There is no destructive principle in Nature, for Nature throughout is pure, unclouded life. Death does not kill; the more living life which has hitherto been concealed bursts forth into new development. Death and birth are but the struggle of life with itself to assume a more glorious and congenial form. And how can *my* death be anything else? For I am not a mere show and semblance of life, but bear within me the one original, true, and essential life. It is impossible to conceive that Nature should annihilate a life which does not proceed from her; I do not exist for Nature, but Nature exists for me.

Even my natural life, even this mere outward manifestation to mortal sight of the inward invisible life, Nature cannot destroy without destroying herself; she who only exists for me, and on account of me, and exists not if I am not. If she destroys me she must animate me anew; for it is only my Higher Life, unfolding itself in her, before which my present life can disappear; and what mortals call death is the visible appearance of this second life. Did no reasonable being who had once beheld the light of this world die, there would be no ground to look with faith for a new heaven and a new earth; the only possible purpose of Nature, to manifest and maintain Reason, would be fulfilled here below, and her circle would be completed. But the very act by which she consigns a free and independent being to death is her own solemn entrance, intelligible to all Reason, into a region beyond this act itself, and beyond the whole sphere of existence which is thereby closed. Death is the ladder by which my spiritual vision rises to a new Life and a new Nature.

When one of my fellow creatures leaves this earthly community, my spirit cannot regard him as annihilated—for he is my fellow creature. My thoughts are drawn to him above: he *is,* and to him there belongs a place. While we mourn for him here below, as in the dim realms of unconsciousness there might be mourning when a man bursts from them into the light of this world's sun, there is rejoicing above that a man is born into that world, as we citizens of the earth receive with joy those who are born unto us. When I shall one day follow, it will be but joy for me; sorrow shall remain behind in the sphere I shall have left.

The world on which but now I gazed with wonder passes away before me and is withdrawn from my sight. With all the fullness of life, order, and increase which I beheld in it, it is yet but the curtain by which a world infinitely more perfect is concealed from me, and the germ from which that other world shall develop itself. My faith looks behind this veil, and cherishes and animates this germ. It sees nothing definite, but it awaits more than it can conceive here below, more than it will ever be able to conceive in all time.

Thus do I live, thus am I, and thus am I unchangeable, firm, and completed for all Eternity; for this is no existence assumed from without—it is my own, true, essential life and being.